Heaven Sent

True Stories of Pets That Have Touched Our Hearts in Miraculous Ways

Compiled by Shanda Trofe
Foreword by Pam Baren Kaplan

**With Twenty-Two Animal-Loving Authors
from Around the Globe**

HEAVEN SENT

Transcendent Publishing
P.O. Box 66202
St. Pete Beach, FL 33736
www.trancendentpublishing.com

Transcendent
Publishing

ISBN: 978-1-7332773-7-2

Library of Congress Control Number:2019954512

Printed in the United States of America.

"Until one has loved an animal, a part of one's soul remains unawakened."

–Anatole France

CONTENTS

Foreword

When the Right Time is Near, the Right Love Will Appear

Pam Baren Kaplan

Zuzu

*W*hen asked to write the foreword for this book, I eagerly accepted without a wag of a tail. I firmly believe our pets are sent from above. How do I know? Faith, though, I do have proof to support my belief. I'd like to tell you my story, or as we say in my Paws to Celebrate Pack, my *tail*.

Unconditional love of fur-family is real and deep. When you lose this member of your family, it's downright devastating.

At thirty-seven years of age, I finally got my wish, a yellow Lab we named Roxy. She was my baby, my sidekick, my walking partner, my everything. Roxy and I loved evening walks. We spent many hours *padding the pavement* over the years, until my girl began showing signs of aging. Arthritis set in, and she was getting weaker. Walking had to be replaced with a less strenuous adventure - lounging in the backyard. That was okay, so long as we were together.

Reflecting back, time was good to Roxy. She passed on January 31, 2011, just shy of her seventeenth birthday, a long loving life for a Lab. The day I lost Roxy was the worst day of my life, even worse than when either of my parents had passed. That day, I lost the most special love of my life.

Depression moved in and the entire family was lost in grief. We barely spoke to each other, let alone in full sentences. Nothing mattered. Things that were once enjoyable, now were meaningless. I missed my Roxy something fierce. The once vibrant color of life shifted to drab.

Months passed. One Sunday morning in early April, my husband and I finally acknowledged each other's existence. He declared, "I don't know about you, but I am really missing a dog."

His words liberated months of pent-up sadness.

"Me too!" I cried. We embraced with meaning for the first time since Roxy passed, then spent the next two hours talking excitedly about getting a new dog. That's when a familiar voice, self-doubt, crept in. "Are you *sure* this is the right time to get another dog?" it said, "You *know* Dani (our daughter) will not welcome a new dog after her BFF has just passed?" And the biggie, "Don't you feel like this is a *betrayal* to Roxy's memory?" The last words rang especially true. I felt guilty and torn between not wanting to betray my love and my desperate need to heal my heart.

I decided I had to sleep on this, only to find that I couldn't. Night after night, my brain kept me up, trying to arrive at the right decision. I was becoming sleep deprived. One night I found myself mumbling in the dark, "Roxy, you know how much we miss you; it's awful without you! I have so much love bottled up inside me with nowhere to go. It's going to explode if my love doesn't get a target!" And then, I asked, "Please send us a puppy, the right puppy, one that you completely approve of. And I promise, you will never, ever be replaced and certainly never forgotten."

This became my mantra. Whenever I had a quiet moment, I'd *converse* with Roxy. Same request, many times over and over. I think I was driving her crazy because there was a shift, a change. I received a call from one of the breeders I had reached out to a while back. A litter was going to be born in late July, all chocolates. He told me if we got our deposit in early the next week, we could have first pick of the females. Without consulting with my husband, I committed to the breeder, "Yes! The check is in the mail!" I got a tingle in my chest and looked up and smiled. "Roxy, I know this is your doing!" I said, and I believed it. It felt right, absolutely right.

Waiting for the pups to be born felt like watching paint dry; time crawled by ever so slowly. I reminded myself that life would be renewed in the family and patience would be rewarded. I had to keep my enthusiasm on low because I didn't want Roxy to think I was going overboard, but my heart was happy in a way that it hadn't been for a long time.

Zuzu was born on July 27, during a big thunderstorm that seemed to announce her arrival. She was one of five girls, and one of the biggest pups in the litter of ten. Now began the seven-week wait before we could bring her home. More patience required.

Gotcha Day finally arrived on September 17, 2011. Zuzu was a bundle of chocolate brown, like a baby bear cub. She was a little more independent than her other four sisters. She also had "Lab-attude," which I fell in love with instantly. She was *deceivingly* calm. Not once did she cry on our three-hour ride home.

From the moment we got home, she took custody of my heart. On her first day she amazed us all when she pawed the patio door to go out to pee!

"She's brilliant!" I announced in a proud mama voice. Zuzu never had a peeing accident in the house! Poop, well that took a bit longer.

She was high energy, even by puppy standards. My daughter referred to her as the "Emotional Terrorist." Why? She was crazy! Not only rambunctious, she was a voracious chewer with expensive taste. She chewed right through my brand-new Audi TT Roadster convertible's seatbelts in what seemed like seconds while on our way to her first obedience class. She didn't chill until nine p.m. each night, that magical hour when her internal clock shut off, only to start up again at six a.m. the next morning. She was exasperating. There were a few times I questioned that *deal* I made with Roxy.

"Is this a little joke you're playing on Mama?" I asked as I looked heavenward, "She's absolutely nuts, but, I don't care, I'm in love!"

A few days had passed, and in a rare moment of *Zuzu calm*, I saw it: the validation of my gift. At the base of Zuzu's chocolate tail was a chunk of yellow fur! I called my husband in to see that I wasn't imagining this. And there it was. I got that same tingle in my chest, and I told my husband, "This is our *heavenly gift* from Roxy, the one I prayed for."

Smiling, he admitted that he too had been *negotiating* with our girl to send us a puppy. "I felt guilty after Roxy passed, like I didn't show her enough love. I promised if she'd send us a puppy I'd love this puppy so much to make it up to her."

We held little Zuzu in our arms, gratefully admiring that chunk of yellow fur. We both believe this is Roxy's signature as she pushed Zuzu from heaven to make sure we would know she was heaven sent.

Pam Baren Kaplan

Pam Baren Kaplan is the bestselling author of *Tails of Unconditional Love, Your Journey to the Other Side of Grief*, memorial jewelry designer and certified professional pet loss grief recovery and life coach.

In August 2015, she founded Paws to Celebrate Pack, a highly interactive, supportive and healing global community for grieving pet parents as they work through the loss of their 4-legger loves.

Previously, Pam spent over three decades in corporate client and employee development, human resources, operations and project management. An emergency triple bypass changed the course of her life, leading Pam to devote her life's purpose and passion to helping people and animals.

In addition to coaching clients worldwide, she continues to serve as *Leader of The Pack* of Paws to Celebrate. She creates handmade memorial jewelry using the ashes of her clients' beloved pets-in-spirit. Her signature piece is, *The Tree of Unconditional Love*. Pam lives in the suburban Chicago area with her husband and two 4-legger girls; Zuzu and Frankie.

Introduction

The Inspiration Behind This Project

Shanda Trofe

My angels in fur coats, Tucker and Lola

I've always held the belief that animals are angels sent from heaven. They come to us at the exact right moment, even if we can't clearly see their purpose at the time. In fact, I'm willing to bet that if you looked back on the animals that have blessed your own life you might realize that they showed up when, or just before, you needed them most.

Perhaps they acted as a support system as you experienced a loss or a hardship or lived through a milestone; perhaps they added levity when you were taking things a bit too seriously. Sometimes it is so subtle we don't make the correlation, and that's okay, too. Just having animals around can offer more healing than some of us even consider or will ever know.

Oftentimes, animals will find us when we aren't even looking. They come into our lives in need of love and care, and we find ourselves stepping out of our own busy routines to nurture them. Animals are clever like that, aren't they? Many come disguised as strays or rescues to grab our attention. The funny thing is, we think we are rescuing them, when in actuality they are rescuing us right back. Sometimes, we simply feel a strong desire to bring a pet into our lives and we'll seek out our little angel, which was the case with both of my dogs.

I am blessed with the love and affection of two dachshunds, and before I got each I felt a strong urge out of nowhere—a knowing—that it was time to bring a dog into our home. I knew their names before I ever saw their faces, and I searched through hundreds of dog pictures looking for the "eyes." I said before finding each, "I'll know by the eyes if it's my dog." And I did! The connection was not only instantaneous, but familiar, as if we had known each other for many lifetimes. Again, this wasn't just a feeling, but a knowing so strong that I traveled great distances to get each of them.

And the moment I met them in person? It's an indescribable feeling to look into your pet's eyes for the first time. It's as if they are transmitting to us, "There you are; I've been waiting for you."

Lola, my female doxie, has been with me for ten years now. She is my best bud, my child, that once-in-a-lifetime dog you'll never forget—she is my everything. Lola never leaves my side, and if she can find her way onto my lap, she claims her spot immediately. She's tuned in to my emotions and knows just when I'm working too hard and need to take a break. She'll even come get me from the computer when I've been spending too much time in front of it. She'll put her little paws on my leg—her gentle reminder that it's time to take a break. Over the years, I've learned that her body echoes mine, and when I'm overworking myself and lacking self-care, it affects her health. Once I made this realization, I became more mindful of my health by incorporating self-care into my daily routine. She's been a great teacher for me in that regard.

Tucker, a younger male doxie, has been with my husband and me for five years now. Unlike Lola, who seems to embody the wisdom of the ages, I believe Tucker is a new soul. Everything is fresh and exciting to him, and he brings an energy into our home that never existed before. He's even helped Lola find her playful side again, and the two not only fill us both with unconditional love, but they love each other just the same. There are few things more beautiful to behold than the love between animals.

Tucker is also a powerful healer, much like my husband, and in fact, seems to mirror him, which is interesting to witness. Each day, the little guy goes to work cleaning up any energy that needs to be cleared from either of us or our home, and he always knows when something is ailing us and is quick to try to fix it. I have a sneaking suspicion that Tucker's offering Reiki, but it's the personality, joy and laughter he brings to our home that's the best medicine of all.

I always tell Lola and Tucker that they are angels sent from heaven to bring us love and joy, and I think they know I'm teasing when I say that God put their wings on their heads and called them ears! All joking aside, I know in my heart our animals are sent from above. They are our healers, our teachers and our most loyal supporters.

Animals are the inspiration behind *Heaven Sent.*

Just as I had felt a strong desire to seek out my dogs, I felt called to create this project. It started with a clear vision that came to me one day and planted itself in my heart. I knew exactly how I wanted the cover to look and what types of stories I wanted to include. I also knew I wanted to give back to the animals for all the unconditional love they offer us, and so I decided all royalties would go to an animal charity chosen by the contributing authors. Finally, I just *knew* this vision was going to continue pulling at my heart until I brought it to fruition. Being a publisher, I had the resources and skills to make this idea come to life, so how could I deny that calling?

As I prepared to announce this project to the world, I felt that special kind of excitement you feel when you know you're doing exactly what you're meant to do, exactly when you're meant to do it. However, nothing could have prepared me for the overwhelming response I received. Each available spot began to fill quickly with pet lovers who had that same strong knowing that they needed to participate in this project. I've never had a multi-author compilation fill up so fast, and I was blown away when I began reading the submissions.

Each story in this book is unique and will tug at your heartstrings in the best possible way. You'll laugh, you'll cry, but my hope is that you'll find the blessing in each story you read and begin to notice how the animals that you come across in your own life are more than just furry friends. They have feelings, they deserve our care, and they deserve our love in return.

Animals don't have many expectations of us, they just love us unconditionally; they give of themselves so freely. These stories will strongly resonate with those who are blessed to have the love of an animal, and I wouldn't be surprised if they awaken some new animal lovers as well.

Each chapter in this book is a testimony to my claim that animals are sent from above. As you read through these pages, I feel confident you'll see that each of these animals—*and authors*—were heaven sent.

Shanda Trofe

Shanda Trofe is a publisher and author coach specializing in book-writing and marketing strategies for authors, coaches, healers and entrepreneurs.

Her passion lies in helping those who are called to share a message with the world to find their voice and connect to their authentic, heartfelt story. She believes that a life rich with experience makes for a great message, and she enjoys working with authors throughout the entire process, from idea to publication.

As the Founder of *Spiritual Writers Network* and President & CEO of *Transcendent Publishing*, Shanda has been helping authors realize their writing and publishing goals since 2012.

She is the author of several books including *Write from the Heart* and *Authorpreneur: How to Build an Empire and Become the AUTHOR-ity in Your Business*. Additionally, she has three romance novels published under her pen name.

Shanda resides in Saint Petersburg, Florida with her loving husband and their two fur babies. www.ShandaTrofe.com

Chapter One

A Reason to Live

Jennifer Benton

My angel from heaven, Pacey

"Jennifer Benton line one…"

I was helping a customer and thought I heard my name over the PA system. They never page me at work, though, so I ignored it. A few minutes later, I heard my name again and went to the phone.

"This is Jennifer, how may I help you?"

There was a silence and I thought the person had hung up, then I heard a tentative "Jennifer?"

"Yes…"

"Hi, this is Jane and I work with your mom…"

Her voice was eerily calm and I couldn't figure out why someone from my mom's work was calling me.

"They think your mom had a heart attack and an ambulance is taking her to the hospital. How fast can you make it there?"

Immediately my mind began to spin. This couldn't be real; I had just talked to Mom this morning and everything was fine. I flashed back to the day when I called my mom to tell her that an ambulance was picking up my brother. I remember trying to stay calm amidst the chaos of sirens, flashing lights, curious neighbors as my brother, blue in the face, his eyes rolled back in his head, was loaded onto a gurney. I was ten years old reassuring my mom that everything would be okay.

"Jennifer, are you there?"

I could barely mutter out, "Yes, I am here…"

I felt the situation was more critical than she was saying because I acted the same way when my brother was slipping in and out of consciousness in my dad's arms. My body felt like it was collapsing; my whole world was caving in on me.

Please don't do this to me! I'll do anything, just don't take my mom.

"So, can you leave now?"

By this time, I was sobbing like a child, chest heaving, snot running out my nose and mascara dripping down my face. The drive to the hospital was a blur. I think my angels got me there safely.

The dreaded word I heard that day was cancer, and it was claiming the life of my mom. I am not sure which is worse, watching someone actually die or watching them suffer the effects of chemotherapy. I cried myself to sleep every night, wanting to crawl out of my skin and be anywhere else than the life I was living. On Easter Sunday I held her hand as she took her last breath and I think my heart stopped beating. I heard someone say, "Is she gone?" I begged God to take me instead.

Three weeks after my mom's death, I went back to work. I could barely peel myself out of bed. I had no desire to go on living without her. I couldn't believe that God had taken both my brother and my mom. Everything seemed so dark and unbearable.

On my first day back, I saw a puppy. She was the cutest thing I had ever seen. Her eyes, one blue and one brown, followed me when I walked by. They seemed to be saying, "Please take me with you." I asked around to see if she belonged to anyone. Everyone thought she was a stray so I took her home for my dad so he wouldn't be lonely. In the car, she insisted on sitting on my lap and I could feel how soft her fur was on my skin. Her presence sent a chill through my spine. There was something familiar about this puppy – I felt an unconditional love like I had with my mom. When she put her face close to mine, I noticed she was covered in fleas, so I took her to the vet to be cleaned up.

As I was leaving, she ran after me and jumped on my leg. I heard her saying, "Please don't leave me alone!"

I gave her a big kiss on her nose and said, "Don't worry, I will be back tomorrow!"

Now I had a dilemma: give her to my dad or keep her myself? I worried about being selfish, and if I would be a good mom to the puppy. How could I be, when I wanted to die? Then I remembered the love radiating through my body as I held her. It felt good to focus on someone other than myself. The more I focused on the puppy, the less I wanted to die. That night, I couldn't stop worrying about her, wondering if she was scared, lonely, or thinking that I had abandoned her. I decided to pray and see how I felt in the morning.

I woke up knowing she would be my dog; that she had been sent to me from heaven. I had been in the pits of hell for the last year and Pacey (the name I chose for her) was my first glimmer of hope. Then the doubts returned. *Will you know what to do with her? Will she listen to you? What if she realizes how depressed you are?* I could feel that glimmer of hope being engulfed by a huge cloud of darkness. The demons were back eating at my soul. How do you stop the never-ending chatter that is crushing every part of your being? It seemed like my depression wanted to keep me stuck. It was like wading into quicksand and unable to get out. Then I thought, there had to be a reason this puppy chose me, that she was in the schoolyard on the day I returned to work after my mom's death. People always laugh when I say I believe in miracles, but there was something special about this puppy; she had an energy of peace and unconditional love that connected directly to my heart.

Pacey was my reason for waking up that first summer without my mom. I decided to crate her (that's what my parents had always done), only to come home one day to find that she had walked the crate off the bottom tray and over to my bed, where she proceeded to destroy my Ralph Lauren bedspread. She was clearly taking a stand on the crating situation and she meant business. After that, Pacey had the run of the apartment.

Pacey had separation anxiety and I couldn't help but wonder if she was mirroring my anxiety over the loss of my mom. Whatever it was, Pacey continued to keep me preoccupied with her shenanigans.

One night I came home and saw a dog in the outside hallway of my building. My first thought was, where is their owner? I looked a little closer and couldn't believe my eyes. Pacey! How had she gotten out? Had I forgotten to close the door?

"Pacey!" I yelled, and she came running down the hallway and covered me with wet, sloppy dog kisses. Pacey seemed really proud of herself for finding me and she expected me to feel the same. I was completely baffled by the situation. When we arrived at my apartment door, it was unlocked. I couldn't believe it, I never leave the house with the door unlocked, even if I am just walking back and forth unloading groceries. Was I in such a fog of grief that I was being reckless? What if Pacey had gotten into the street and was hit by a car? In the months after my mom's passing, it was easier to imagine the worst scenario. It was as if an entity took over my brain, sending me into a never-ending tunnel of doom. The battle in my mind stopped when Pacey jumped up and touched my shoulder with her paw. The one thing I knew in that moment was I absolutely loved this dog. She was definitely my angel, my reason to continue living.

Pacey and I went inside to find a message from a neighbor on the machine. She sounded really upset.

"I found your dog and brought her in my apartment," she said. "I went to do laundry and YOUR dog locked me out. When she finally unlocked the door, I put her back in the hallway. Good luck finding her."

I looked at Pacey and said, "Really, you left the apartment without Kylie?"

Kylie was my cat.

I then fell on the floor laughing, and Pacey came over and licked my face. I hoped she didn't think I was condoning her behavior, but she must have, because the next day she locked me out! I called the police (they didn't feel it was an emergency) and building management (no one answered), then realized my best option was to sit outside and talk Pacey into unlocking the door.

After two hours, Pacey decided to let me inside and I started looking for a doggie daycare. Geez, looking at the prices, I figured Pacey would come home knowing how to read and write!

On Pacey's first day, I arrived to pick her up and saw she was in front with the employees. Oh no, she must be in trouble.

Instead, they said, "Watch this." It was a video of the dogs running around the room. Then out of nowhere, Pacey jumped up and opened the door to let the dogs escape!

Pacey always kept me on my toes, which was a great distraction from my depression. One of her favorite entrees was cat poop sprinkled with litter. One day she decided to change it up and I came home to clumping cat litter spread evenly across my kitchen floor. I am not sure how long I laid on the floor crying, but I do know Pacey was by my side the entire time. Finally, I got up to clean it and I started laughing. How did she spread the litter so perfectly? It was like a work of art!

I could swear Pacey was human; sometimes, I even thought she was my mom and brother reincarnated to mess with me. At the very least, they were laughing in heaven.

Pacey and I loved to ride in my convertible. Top down, fur and hair blowing in the wind. She tolerated her seatbelt but wanted nothing to do with her doogles (I thought they were cool because they matched my car). Our favorite car ride was to the lake. Pacey loved running through the woods and cruising on the paddleboat, except for the time it started to sink. She crawled up to the tip of the boat, the only part that wasn't in the water, while I frantically tried to right the craft.

It was during an adventure at the lake that I realized Pacey would soon be going home to be with my mom and brother. I let her run in the woods as usual, but when by dusk she hadn't returned I became nervous. This wasn't like her; she always came when I called. Normally, the dark woods scared me, but my spirit was aching for Pacey. As I ran barefoot down the wooded hill after her, my toe caught in the brush and I fell to the ground face first. There was a throbbing pain in my foot and when I rolled over to check the damage, I saw I was gushing blood. As I lay there, all I could think of was, "Please God, don't take Pacey!" The darkness started closing in on me as I feared the worst. I felt disconnected from my mind, like I was watching this happen to someone else.

The sound of a dog whimper startled me, bringing me back into my body. I turned my head and saw Pacey laying a few feet away from me. In the midst of my panic attack, I hadn't noticed her. I scrambled over to Pacey and wrapped my arms around her. I never wanted to let go.

After that night, Pacey's hind legs gave out more often. It became a battle to carry her down the stairs, so I moved to a first-floor apartment. I bought Pacey a plush memory foam bed and when she continued to jump in my bed, I started sleeping on the floor with her. I knew the dreaded day was coming and I couldn't do anything to stop it. My angel who had kept me alive for sixteen years after my mom's death was telling me it was time for her to go. Holding Pacey that last night felt like I was losing a part of my soul. She was my life line and it was being severed. Death is peculiar; they say you go to a better place, yet the journey can be filled with pain and the people left behind are devastated.

My best friend drove me and Pacey to the emergency vet. I wrapped Pacey in a green blanket and loved on her the whole way.

When the vet opened the door, Pacey popped her head up to make sure everything was okay, then rested her head back on my arm.

"Are you ready?" the vet asked. I wanted to scoop Pacey up and run away as fast as I could. I wanted to yell out, "No, life isn't fair!" "This world sucks!" "Not again, God!" Instead, I just gave a slight nod of my head. I heard him explaining what would happen and I kept my eyes on Pacey. The vet left and I laid my head next to hers, letting her know how much I cherished her. I think I would have stayed there forever if my friend didn't come in to get me.

As I said, death is strange; when you lose a loved one your entire world is shattered and you want things to stop for a while so you can process everything. The truth is nothing stops, everything keeps going, and no one notices you are dying inside. You want to scream out for help but figure no one will understand anyway. You wonder if you look different because surely all the pain you are feeling on the inside is seeping through to the outside. Can't anyone see it?

Everyone said, "Oh, look how good she is doing." I wanted to whisper, "Come a little closer, I don't think you're seeing me clearly."

To Pacey, I was transparent; she sensed my pain through my energy. She knew part of me was dying and her mission was to save my life. I don't believe in coincidences and I know Pacey was sent here for me. She loved me unconditionally, just like my mom. Reminding me that love never dies. No matter where we are in this Universe, you can feel the energy of love. You might not always see the wings, but you definitely know when you've been blessed with an angel.

Jennifer Benton

Jennifer Benton is a teacher, energy worker and life coach. She holds a Bachelor of Arts in journalism with an emphasis in advertising and a minor in business, as well as two masters degrees in School and Professional Counseling, and has been trained in Bioenergetics Therapy and Artist of the Spirit Life Coaching. Jennifer has taught first and second grade and special education, and spent ten years as a school counselor.

Three years ago, Jennifer took a leap of faith, packed everything that would fit in her Mustang convertible and drove from Texas to Oregon to begin a new chapter in her life. She enjoys hiking, biking, kayaking, and snowshoeing, but her true passion is helping people reach their full potential. She encourages everyone to look on the inside and bring their unique gifts to the world. She is always looking for new opportunities to help the world become a better place.

Contact:

Jenlynben777@gmail.com

Chapter Two

And God Had a Plan

Margaret-Maggie Honnold

Honnold's Hounds

*T*he council gathered in the large soft grassy area at the foot of the Rainbow Bridge. They stretched in the warm sun and enjoyed the fresh scent of the air. Bowls of clear water and their favorite foods were scattered nearby, but none had been hungry since coming to the Rainbow Bridge. As they talked amongst themselves, each was aware of a quiet buzz of anticipation. St. Francis of Assisi, the patron saint of animals, was coming personally to join them on this most auspicious occasion.

Heinz, the long-haired dachshund, saw him first and rushed to meet him, his short furry legs tangling in St. Francis' long flowing robes. The birds twittered and laughed. St. Francis reached to snuggle Heinz, telling him, "It is a good thing I have my staff ready when you run to meet me, or we would both have a roll in the grass."

In short order, the rest of the pack came to greet him with doggie kisses and tail wags. St. Francis greeted each of them as a treasured friend, then they all turned to look at the Rainbow Bridge.

Today was April 29, 2010 on Earth and there were some big changes coming to their old home and to their momma Maggie's life. They were prepared. A committee of Heinz, Murray and Emmy had gotten the buffet ready. Lucky, Beau, Muggins and Mickey had made the welcome signs. Princess was dressed in her finest ruby-encrusted collar and matching scarf. Now they just waited. Two more of their Momma's heart dogs would be coming to the bridge soon.

"It is happening," St. Francis said after a few moments, "Get ready."

The little pack jumped to their feet and rushed to stand at the foot of the Rainbow Bridge, their hearts open, their eyes watching expectantly.

Looking slightly confused and bedraggled and smelling of smoke, Basset Hounds Hollyberry and Brudder Noah came slowly across the bridge.

Princess ran forward first. She gave Holly a tender sniff and told her, "You took my place when I came to the bridge. Thank you for taking such good care of our Momma."

She then turned to Noah and welcomed him by gently washing his smoke-covered face with her soft tongue.

"We all saw you cuddling with Momma this morning, none of you knew what was instore for our pack today. But it will all be okay, for there is a great and good plan that Father God has for all His children and animals alike. In fact, ThelmaLou, who will join our pack next, is already on her way to Momma's heart. Come on, let's get you cleaned up and enjoy the feast that is set out just for you."

They headed into the land of the Rainbow Bridge to commune and watch what Father God had planned to help Momma heal her heart and go forward.

Momma's good friend Jan had been shocked and deeply saddened when she heard of the fire at Maggie's house and the loss of her animals and possessions. The two women had become acquainted when Jan helped Maggie adopt Noah from a Basset rescue and quickly bonded over their love of dogs. Jan had given Maggie invaluable advice and had even been a guest in their home.

Jan was heavily involved with animal rescue, so when the call came Jan hurried to pull ThelmaLou, another abandoned Basset Hound, from a local kill shelter. The petite red and white girl was past her euthanasia date, but the staff liked her so much they persisted in trying to find a home for her. She had come into rescue on April 29, 2010. It was unusual to make a dispensation for an animal in a kill shelter, but "TL" was an exception.

TL went home with Jan and waited once more to see where she would end up. Just three years old, she had already been in two homes.

But God had a plan.

TL would get another reprieve when she overstayed her time in foster care with Jan, but Jan knew TL was the one for Maggie. April 29, 2010 was a date they all would remember.

Maggie signed the adoption papers, a friend "gifted" Maggie by paying the adoption fee and Jan let TL stay at her house until Maggie's new home was completed. On delivery day Jan watched as Maggie buried her face in Thelma's silky ears and began to cry. Thelma cuddled her soft snout into Maggie's neck. As mourning and thankfulness blended, Jan knew she was following the plan.

The pack watched from the bridge as TL settled into her new home. It wouldn't be long, they knew, before the next leg of God's plan went into action.

Momma had lost two dogs in the fire and her home still felt a little empty. The pack was not one bit surprised when out of the blue another friend showed up at her front door with a Basset Hound who needed a home.

St. Francis had laughed and laughed when he saw this development. Father God's plans are so good!

"Watch this, everyone," he said in an almost mischievous tone, like someone holding on to a good secret but anxious to share it.

The pack barked in anticipation.

"Where did he come from?" they heard their Momma ask.

"Well, from Terre Haute, but originally he came from a breeder south of Marshall. He was born November 4, 2008 and has had two different homes."

Momma's eyes filled with tears. Holly, one of the dogs lost in the fire, had also been born on that date, and she had come from a breeder south of Marshall. She looked down at this new sweet face and, thinking he could be Holly's brother, decided to call him Huckleberry. After giving him a big welcoming hug, she gave him a bath, fed him, clipped his nails and introduced him to TL and Dad. Honnold's Hounds were filling in with connections that were beyond coincidence.

Time passed and a daily routine developed at Honnold's Hounds. Fences were in place, grandkids came and went, Dad continued to walk the Alzheimer's path and Huck became his partner. Huck made it a rule to never leave Dad's side. He slept with him, sat on the floor by his chair, shared Dad's cookies and licked his face and hands. Huck often comforted Dad when he could feel his sadness.

The following March Momma came home with another surprise: Holly and Huck's breeder was going out of business, and she had one older female dog that no one wanted. She would give her to Momma, if Momma would just come and get her. The Rainbow Bridge gang held their breath. They knew Phoebe's Mourning had lived a very confined life. God had a plan for her to come to a family who would love her, let her run and be part of the hound pack.

They watched as Momma and her granddaughter, the same one who had brought Holly to Momma, went and "rescued" Phoebe. They cheered and Phoebe barked as the car pulled onto the highway heading home. God had a plan for both Phoebe and Momma to have someone else to care for.

Just as she had with Huck, Momma gently took the old basset hound and bathed her, clipped her nails, put a fresh, clean collar around her chafed neck and showed her where her food and water bowls were located. They watched as Momma looked into Phoebe's soft brown eyes and gently rubbed her ears, saying to her, "No more mourning for you, old girl, we are just going to call you Gramma Phoebe because you are the senior member of this pack."

Gramma Phoebe settled into her new home. Afraid of men, she stuck close to Momma. The pack watched from the Rainbow Bridge as Momma made her a soft bed at her feet. Gramma supervised Momma's writing, becoming her muse. The pack had laughed and cheered when Momma began to write once more.

God had a plan.

Dad's condition continued to deteriorate, and the hounds became more and more supportive of their Momma, taking turns sleeping with her and sitting at her feet and licking her tears.

God's plan then set "the puppy cure" in motion.

Fergus was one of four pups born to a female Basset Hound in a rescue in Arkansas. Momma's friend Menzie helped birth the litter and kept them until they were ready for forever homes. For Fergus, that meant a move to Illinois to join Honnold Hound's ever-growing family.

It was decided that although Fergus' mother was full-blooded Basset his father was a traveling salesman of the Black and Tan Bloodhound variety. Fergus had the personality of a Bloodhound – sweet and affectionate. He also ate everything in sight: eyeglasses, light cords, shoes, potato chips, and of course, his toys. Unfortunately, as it often is with rescue dogs, Fergus was not healthy from the beginning and the very hard decision was made to have him join the other hounds at the Rainbow Bridge. This was fine with Fergus, who loved to play party games and gladly joined in the pack's festivities as they gathered at the bridge. As for St. Francis and the others, well, they just looked at each other, wondering what God would do next.

Dad moved to the nursing home, and Momma continued her volunteer job transporting Basset Hounds. One day she got a call to pick up a female basset who had been found on the street. This beautiful red gal needed a foster home while she completed her rehab and healing before going to a forever home.

Momma, her daughter Monica and TL went to get her. TL didn't particularly like her, but Momma and Monica fell in love with her. Momma named her RozElynne. She came as a foster but stayed forever, becoming fast friends with Gramma Phoebe.

God had a plan.

Changes started coming faster now. Dad entered a hospital far away and Momma retired from her job and moved with him. The Bassets visited him in the hospital, they supported Momma, and they once more lost count of how many tears she cried into their soft necks and ears, but God didn't.

Eventually, Dad went to Heaven and the entire group ran to meet him, including all the animals he had loved over the years - dogs, cats, horses… the party went on for hours.

Things on Earth did not go as smoothly. TL had to have surgery on her eyes that rendered her blind, but she still loved her backyard. Gramma helped guide her and Momma stopped rearranging the furniture so TL could get around.

One day, Gramma suddenly started having trouble breathing. The vet found a large tumor blocking her airway and within a short time she too had made her trip to the bridge. She was greeted with the same loving enthusiasm as all the hounds had been greeted. When she arrived she was given her assignment: she was going to watch over TL.

Momma was surprised one day when after giving TL a treat she saw the dog go racing into Momma's bedroom. When she followed, she found TL trying to bury her treat in the corner of the closet. Momma took a picture of her and upon looking at it closely could see a white sphere floating just inside the closet. As Momma laughed, the group at the bridge looked at one another in confusion. Gramma explained that this was the spot where she used to bury her own treats. Momma had seen the white sphere and knew Gramma was supervising. The hounds at the bridge high-fived Gramma; she had made Momma happy.

Life continued and everyone aged until one day it was apparent that TL was very sick. Despite medical care and much love, it was her time for the bridge. With Momma holding her in her arms, and Huck and RozE standing close to Momma, Thelma arooooed a final good-bye with her signature twenty-seven howls.

The ashes of TL and Gramma now rest in Basset Hound cookie jars on Momma's bookshelf, keeping her company when she writes. Huck spends most of his time lying on Momma's right foot and RozE sleeps on the dog bed behind Momma's desk chair. Though they too are aging now they still look after Momma.

And God still has a plan.

DazE Honnold joined Honnold's Hounds on February 3, 2019. She is a Black and Tan Bloodhound puppy born on November 2, 2019. November 2 was Dad's earthly birthday. DazE has completed the pack for now. She looks just like Fergus, only with longer legs, and she is as loving and mischievous as he was.

Never doubt the love that spreads from the heart of a dog to the heart of his human. It is a God's gift bond.

I am a God's Gift Dog
by Hollyberry

My Momma calls me a "God Dog" for she had made it known, that before I came to her house her heart was made of stone.

She'd cried and cried since her Princess died and she said she was so sad, that she no wanted another dog, no way, no how, too bad (she wanted a new living room rug instead).

But Jesus, had another plan for He is all 'bout love, and who can help Him to spread that care from our Father up above.

God's plans are great and kind and good, and in wisdom He did know, just what would turn one heart aflame and return to it its glow.

He knows it's man's best friend He does, that a gentle, loving pup can get inside and melt a heart before it knows what's up.

With a few wet licks, a wagging tail, a snooter kiss or two, a cold, cold heart will warm right up with love that is brand new.

My Momma says God's everywhere, and He works in many ways and puppies are just one of those and it won't take many days,

For a little long-nosed puppy with droopy ears and eyes, to make those tears all dry up, but not to God's surprise.

For dogs are His creation, made with love and care and He gave them a loving nature with everyone to share (Momma says that's just like God himself).

So, who can get into a stone-cold heart before one knows what's up? A tiny, little Basset Hound, a spanking brand-new pup.

Thank you, Heavenly Father, for making me, Hollyberry, a great "Christ"mas gift.

You had a plan.

Margaret-Maggie Honnold

Margaret-Maggie Honnold lives in a small midwestern town adjacent to the Mississippi River. Retired now, she spends much of her time writing about her experiences as a registered nurse, health educator, widow, mother, grandmother, former Alzheimer's caregiver and animal lover. A graduate of Kankakee Community College and Eastern Illinois University with degrees in Nursing and Health Education, she has worked in both the hospital and community health settings, enabling her to write insightfully of life's circumstances.

Margret-Maggie volunteers as an Elder in her church and serves as a board member on the Kibbe Historical Museum and Hearts of Hancock Humane Society. Best of all, she loves to cuddle with her two Basset Hounds and Bloodhound puppy or take her camera and wander the countryside.

Her book, *The Cloisonné Heart,* was a #1 Amazon best seller and a Finalist in the International Book Awards for 2018. She has contributed to several compilation books, all of which are available on Amazon. Her exclusive collection of poetry & prose picture books, as well as a variety of cards and photography prints, can be purchased privately.

Contact her on Facebook at Margaret-Maggie Honnold, Author.

Or her website at www.margarethonnold.com

Email at machonnold@outlook.com

Chapter Three

Angel Blue Eyes

Lisa A. Clayton

Indigo Mystic: Angel Blue Eyes of Heart Love and Healing

*W*e all receive heaven-sent messages, whether we realize it or not. Sometimes these messages are very subtle, other times they keep appearing in our lives until we take notice. I call these repeating messages "Angel wake-up calls."

In the fall of 2013, I was experiencing a profound sense of unrest and uneasiness. Not only was I was rebuilding my business from a financial quagmire, I had broken away from long-term relationships and was feeling more alone than ever.

As I tried to figure out my life, my intuition kept nagging me to share my unique Angel connections and gifted intuitive abilities as my life service. Why did I keep relying on corporate training contracts to sustain my living when they could end abruptly? Why did I keep repeating this cycle over and over? I needed an Angel wake-up call!

One day, feeling restless, lost and lonely, I was walking in the quaint downtown area of Half Moon Bay, California when I saw a couple sitting with their dog, a miniature schnauzer that bore a striking resemblance to my precious Dixie Doodle. Dixie, who had been my true soul companion, had left this world in 2000, the same time I was going through a divorce and a move to a second-floor condo. Though I missed having a pet, I decided it would be unfair to bring another into this living situation, where it would have no yard or space to roam free, not to mention my frequent absences due to business commitments and travel. Plus, how could my heart ever heal from the deep loss of losing Dixie?

That had been thirteen years ago, yet seeing this couple and their schnauzer reminded me how much I missed Dixie and the joy of being a pet parent. I approached them and with an aching heart shared my Dixie Doodle story. When they remarked that perhaps this was a sign, I firmly explained that my current living and work situations prevented me from getting another animal.

The very next day as I was enjoying my morning coffee at an outside café, another miniature schnauzer ran up to me, wagging joyfully. How ironic it was to share my Dixie love story once again with her owners! My heart filled with a piercing nostalgia that sparked an intense stirring and a feeling of wonderment. What was going on?

On the third day, I was grabbing a quick lunch at a local diner when I witnessed an elderly woman desperately trying to open her van door. As I approached to help, she expressed relief and gratitude – she needed to retrieve her fur baby from her van, she said, as the afternoon temperature was rising.

"If your fur baby is a miniature schnauzer," I remarked, "I will do a back flip in this parking lot."

She giggled and shouted, "Start warming up!" To my surprise, another miniature schnauzer greeted me with love licks and wiggles.

I shared with this beautiful blue-eyed lady the "coincidental" schnauzer sightings of the past three days. When I added that they all reminded me of my beloved Dixie Doodle, she gave me an intense look.

"Lisa," she whispered, "there is a puppy calling you."

"Oh no, it's not possible!" I exclaimed, then proceeded to go down my list of excuses as to why a pet was not an option for me. The woman's crystal blue eyes penetrated mine as she took my hand in hers and squeezed tightly.

"Lisa, there is a puppy calling you NOW. These encounters are Angel wake-up calls for you to take action."

I was visibly shaken as I said goodbye to the woman, and my emotions were still running rampant that night as I tossed and turned. Finally I fell into a deep sleep, only to awake again at 3:33 – no surprise as Angels wake me up often with "time signs." I was guided to turn on my computer and search miniature schnauzers in California. And there, on the first page that popped up, was a blue-eyed schnauzer pup. My heart was beating furiously as I pieced together the signs.

My father had blue eyes. His eyes were the only organ he could donate from his cancer-riddled body when he died, exactly one year after I lost my beloved Dixie. During this time I had also lost a beautiful home, my beloved marriage and job security. My heart had been broken in many pieces very quickly and deeply, and now, as I stared at the pup, I realized that over this thirteen-year timespan my heart had not healed completely from these painful losses.

A blue-eyed woman in the parking lot, my father's blue eyes and now a blue-eyed puppy available on my first search guided at 3:33? Were these signs from the Angels that it was finally time to heal my heart with unconditional love from another animal spirit? Should I reach out and inquire about this blue-eyed pup who appeared to be heaven-sent?

The next morning I arrived at work at a senior living facility. When I showed a picture of the blue-eyed pup to the CEO, he exclaimed, "We will reinstate the pet therapy program and you can lead it."

Wow! Was this another sign to take immediate action?

Later that day I was in my car and decided to call Karyn, the blue-eyed pup's mother. We spent a few minutes interviewing each other, and when she learned I was an ordained Angel minister and did intuitive readings, she exclaimed, "Oh, my son must have sent you to me!" When I asked for more information, she said sadly, "Chase died in Afghanistan during his military tour of duty and my heart has been broken ever since. I started raising puppies with my beloved schnauzers to help heal my heart. Maybe you and the Angels can help me too."

With chills running through me, I almost ran off the road. At that very moment I was passing a "Chase" bank.

The Angel signs were not only synchronistic, they were causing a pounding in my heart so strong with a love connection I hadn't felt in years. I could hardly wait to meet Indigo Mystic, the name I had already given this blue-eyed pup clearly calling me from the Angelic realms.

However, it wasn't Indigo Mystic that brought tears streaming and immediate love to my heart on the day I arrived to meet her. It was her birth mother, Phoebe. Phoebe looked identical to my Dixie and never left my side during my two-hour visit. Karyn, Phoebe's owner, stated she had not seen Phoebe so attached to anyone so intensely and lovingly.

As I looked in Phoebe's eyes, I knew in my intuitive heart and soul that she was Dixie. Phoebe-Dixie was so happy to be with me, especially since I had listened and followed the Angel signs to find her. She was giving me part of her loving soul in a blue-eyed pup to finally heal my heart.

On December 10, 2013, my sister and I journeyed to bring Indigo Mystic to her new home. December 10th is the day my father ascended to light, lending his blue eyes to someone here on earth. My father's blue eyes seemed to be shining through Indigo's blue eyes with her loving spirit on that special day, calling me through the etheric realms to celebrate them both.

When Indigo Mystic arrived in my life, everything changed, especially my life service mission. I started conducting more Angel readings and with each one, Indigo fully tuned in. I realized she had an ability to see and sense Angels and other soul spirits. She is very empathic and reads the energy fields of others so easily, helping me tune in with greater clarity.

Indigo's mission on this planet is to generate pure joy as she greets everyone – children, elders, neighbors, strangers and home-less with passionate excitement to love each person. Our condo living promotes many daily and evening walks, each one an adventure. My heart swells each time and is in amazement as my blue-eyed Angel chooses and greets people who need extra love.

One day we were out for our usual early-morning walk around the neighborhood with Indigo leading our way. There is a particular street Indigo loves to explore, and we were halfway up it when she abruptly turned around and went the opposite way. I did my best to convince her to come back on our familiar trek but she stubbornly refused and ran towards an elderly woman in the crosswalk. Indigo waited eagerly at the corner while the woman slowly crossed and greeted her with yelps and wiggles like finding a long-lost friend.

"How did your Angel dog know?" she said tearfully, "I just lost my beloved pooch of many years and am heartbroken. Your dog is bringing me so much joy, running to me with kisses."

On another morning walk, a group of tough-acting teenage boys were hanging out in front of our nearby middle school, shoving each other and calling each other names. Indigo ran up to them and jumped in the middle of all their pushing and shoving, wagging her tail and yelping happily. Once again, she appeared to have found hearts that needed her love. Each boy immediately stopped their actions and knelt down to pet her. She licked their faces and jumped on their laps.

One boy, who appeared to be the ringleader, remarked, "I've never seen a blue-eyed dog so it must be from God, right?"

I smiled and agreed.

These examples represent only two of the many magical Indigo love stories. She attracts and magnetizes multitudes of people with whom I would never have the opportunity to talk. While we are walking, someone almost always comes up to us and asks to pet Indigo or marvels at her brilliant blue eyes, leading to a joyful and unexpected encounter that human beings, left to their own devices would not experience. When was the last time you approached someone and just started talking to them in a public place? It rarely happens in our busy human lives but in Indigo's life, it is a regular occurrence. She is truly a heart-soul connector who greets each stranger like a long-lost friend.

I am one blessed Mama who receives unexpected Indigo Mystic learnings and wisdom each day. She brings forth wonders and miracles guiding me in my energy work, raising the frequency of love during Angel readings and giving me signs to slow down or speed up my pace in my own life.

Many times in the middle of the night, Indigo will let me know when the Angels and Spirit Guides are near by giving a soft whimper and looking up at the ceiling. I grab my pen and journal and start writing the downloads, as I trust the Indigo-Angel wake-up call to receive important messages from Divine.

When Indigo needs to go outside at unusual times during the night, I realize it is not an inconvenience, but a blessing. There might be a full moon glowing, a comet streaking through the sky or a beautiful natural wonder that I would never experience if I followed my human alarm clock. She senses beautiful sunrises and sunsets and brings me to them. She serves as my weather and nature channel, my link to the extraordinary.

Indigo Mystic brings to this world powerful unconditional love and heart healing with her Angel blue eyes. She begins each day with a determined and adventurous spirit, anticipating who she will meet and greet, knowing love cures and calms all. And believe me, she has indeed healed the holes in my heart that I was holding onto for thirteen long years!

We are never alone. Whether it be an animal spirit like Dixie Doodle or significant others like my dad who have passed on to light, trust they are always sending you Angel signs and guidance. When the signs align with an urgency to act, I hope an animal spirit appears in your life, such as my blue-eyed Angel did for me, healing your heart and filling it with an unconditional love that is heaven-sent.

Lisa A. Clayton

Lisa is an entrepreneur, author, spiritual intuitive and founder of Source Potential, a human evolution learning company. She has more than 35 years of experience in professional consulting, keynote speaking and transformational coaching, which is rooted in her philosophy of "learning from the inside out." Lisa is an ordained Angel minister, specializing in connecting individuals with their Divine Team and inner Source for daily living, as well as a HeartMath® Master Trainer and Licensed Coach, teaching individuals and groups heart techniques for building coherent, compassionate living environments.

Lisa has creatively combined her intuitive abilities with heart-consciousness methods to establish the *Inner Leader Movement* – multidimensional intuitive guidance sessions focused upon harnessing one's inner leader abilities such as power, courage and confidence to elevate his/her unique spiritual gifts and life mission.

Lisa is a contributing author to several books, including *365 Days of Angel Prayers, 111 Morning Meditations* and *52 Weeks of Gratitude Journal.*

lisaaclayton.com

lisa@sourcepotential.com

650-712-0300

Chapter Four

Bella Means Beauty

Rosemary Hurwitz

Sweetheart Bella, always found her comfortable place.

"*O*h, look at this one, Caitlin," I said to my seven-and-a-half-year-old daughter. "She's just beautiful!" As we looked down at the grey with white tabby, she turned her big saucer eyes up to us and stared as if to say, "Yes! I'm the one!" I didn't know whether it was that stare or her beautiful coat, but indeed, she stood out among the many other kittens up for adoption that day at the Orphans of the Storm animal shelter.

Within minutes of being alone with her in the adoption room, Caitlin and I knew we were in love. The kitten's fur felt like the softest velvet, and at five months she was a bit older than a baby so we could see her personality pretty clearly. She was sweet, affectionate and purring loudly, showing her contentment, and her connection to us, already. As we got to know her I felt my spirit lifting for the first time in months. We had lost my dad in August and I had been grieving well into autumn.

After finalizing the adoption, we put the newest member of our family in a box and went to surprise Carly, my other daughter. Carly, who loves cats, was beyond delighted; my husband Dale, on the other hand, was not.

"Isn't she beautiful?" the girls and I asked, trying to win him over. "What if we call her Bella, after your Grandma Belle?"

Immediately, his eyes softened and he reached over to pet her. "Ohhhhh-k," he said and gave us a little smile.

We already had a rather full house, including a Collie named Danny and two other cats, Copper and Cosmo. We all loved the cats, but they each seemed to bond with one family member in particular. Copper was "my" super affectionate orange and white male tabby, and Cosmo, a white Siamese mix who had come to us after my mom passed five years earlier, had "adopted" Carly as his favorite. Time would tell if Bella was also a one-person cat.

About a week or so after bringing Bella home, it was time to get her spayed. When I brought her home after the surgery, she was a little groggy and I looked around for a place for her to rest. Caitlin had a little wooden cradle, a gift from her grandma, where she kept her dolls. Now I turned it into a comfy bed for Bella's recuperation. She fit in it perfectly, and as she snuggled in she seemed grateful to me, as if she sensed I wanted to ease any post-surgery discomfort she felt. Caitlin was elated when she came home from school that day to find not a doll but her new kitten in the cradle. She did a great job being gentle and tending to Bella's needs. I remember this time of Bella's surgery as a teachable moment with the kids, not only about taking care of loved ones, but about the importance of spaying or neutering pets because there were so many animals in the shelters.

As for Bella, she healed quickly and soon became the darling of the household, with her softest charcoal gray mottled fur and the prettiest white surrounding her pink nose, mouth and belly. We would say it looked like she ate a marshmallow that stayed there.

Although Bella was friendly and affectionate with everyone, she soon followed in the footsteps of the other felines in the house. She chose Caitlin as her person and more often than not could be found on the end of our daughter's bed. This would be her pattern for about ten years until Caitlin went off to college.

Bella also loved dogs. She became best buddies with our collie Danny until he passed away from lymphoma, and later welcomed Buddy, the next collie that came into our lives. "Who says dogs and cats don't get along?" we'd say, smiling, whenever we saw her winding her body around Buddy. "Look at Bella, giving the dog love!"

Bella also wound herself around my legs when my beloved Copper passed away; it was if she was saying, "I know you're hurting, and I'm here." Shortly after that, a neighbor asked us if we would welcome a new orange, very fluffy tabby cat. We said yes, and we named him Cam (though the kids nicknamed him Floofy). At first Bella was a bit threatened by this sweet new boy who liked our bed, but being a sweet girl herself, she tolerated him pretty well.

Bella loved the summers at the cottage, sipping from the pure lake water, climbing trees and catching mice. In the fall, when Caitlin and three of her siblings were off at school, Bella looked to me and my husband for comfort, whether it was an early morning snuggle or a walk with the dogs. In the evenings she loved sitting on my husband's chest, tucking her head under his chin. Sometimes she headed off on a mini adventure of her own, but she never went out in the rain and rarely in the snow, and she never went far. If you called her name, she'd soon be at the door.

Whatever the season, Bella always found the most beautiful comfy places to sit. If I got a new comforter for the bed, she'd be on it. Outside on the patio furniture, she'd find the just-cleaned cushions to nest in. The last picture I posted of Bella on Instagram, (#catsofinstagram) was this summer. At our lake cottage, I always have about ten beach towels folded piled high and, sure enough, Bella, like the Princess and the Pea, sat at the top of the pile of towels. (I posted the picture with the hashtags: #PrincessandthePea and #catshaveselfesteem.)

She spent hot sunny days under the deck, coming when she was hungry or thirsty, and when the sun went under the clouds, she would join us on the dock to watch the sunset.

She and Cam slept on the screened in porch or the deck furniture. She loved the outdoors and she was free to use the porch cat door as it prevented her from crafting a "screen cat door"!

Back at home, you could always find Bella in her bed on top of our bedroom cabinet or on our bed. Outside she would lounge on the patio furniture or on our bluestone patio, which kept her cool on a hot day. Wherever we found her she would always be looking up at us with her pretty eyes full of affection. She also said "I love you" by bring me a mouse here and there, to which I would say, "No thank you, Bella. We have enough groceries."

Bella waited until she was sixteen to teach me an important lesson about faith. It was this past summer, and we had been up at our lake in Michigan with all four adult kids and two grandbabies, who came up the first ten days of August.

On the last day of our son's visit, we began the five-and-a-half hour drive back to the Chicago area for a family wedding. When I got back to the lake on Monday evening, our neighbors, who had been caring for our dogs and cats, said they hadn't seen Bella since Sunday evening where they left her on the porch after letting the dogs out.

It was not like Bella to be gone for more than a day; certainly, she came back when we called her name a few times and put her food out. So when on Tuesday morning she still hadn't returned I began to get concerned.

I called her name as I went up and down the street, but no Bella. That night I put her favorite food in our window flower box, which was outside our bedroom window. She would often hop up in the early morning and meow for her food. In the morning I woke up and was sad and alarmed to see the untouched can of food.

I had a funny feeling, so I did an Angel Card reading on the question, "What do I need to know about Bella?" I pulled three cards:

1. *See Only Love* 2. *Reward Yourself* 3. *Joy.*

Could I feel Bella's spirit in this reading? It felt like it, or at least like someone was guiding me from the Divine realm. There was the feeling of "There is no fault here – not with the neighbors, or your family, or Bella. It has all been loving."

From the second card, *Reward Yourself,* I felt a nudge to be good to myself, and to make it a nice vacation for my husband. It felt like the message was, "You are tired from all the company – you give a lot to your family, including your dogs and cats. This is your and husband's vacation now, with no company for five days, so *reward yourself.* It felt odd and yet so right.

Dale and I had been dreaming of replacing our small sailboat that had broken down several years earlier. On Tuesday when I went around calling for Bella, I saw a used Sun Fish sailboat in our neighbor's front yard with a FOR SALE sign on it. We bought it and our neighbor hooked it up to his tractor, brought it over, and even gave Dale a little refresher lesson. That was a bright spot in the week. The *Joy* card, the third one I'd pulled in the reading, spoke to me as though we needed to feel the joy that was all around us even in this sad time without our sweet cat. I felt, too, that somehow Bella was in a state of joy.

Wednesday morning, there was still no Bella. Dale and I called her name and looked all around. With our neighbor's help we posted on several online shelters, and we created laminated posters with the Princess and the Pea photograph and the words "MISSING BELLA," which we put up on telephone poles and in mailboxes. There was no response, and we felt our hearts sinking with each passing day.

On Friday evening I told God that not being certain about what had happened to her was very difficult. "Please send me a sign," I asked, then, trying to hold space for gratitude, I prayed, "Dear God, we are so grateful for her wonderful sixteen years, but especially because she was elderly, and this wasn't like her, I am worried. When you take care of a cat for sixteen years and don't know where it is, it is very hard. I believe you will guide me, so please send a sign."

Not ten minutes after my prayer and search across the street, a lady rode her bike over and said, "I had to stop because I've seen your posters and I saw your cat."

"Oh wonderful!" I exclaimed, feeling a glimmer of hope. "Do you remember when?"

She told me it was hard to say but she thought the sighting was about five nights earlier while she was on her bike.

"That would have been Sunday night when our neighbors last saw Bella," I said, "Does that sound right?"

She said it did.

She then told me she liked to go for a bike ride around nine p.m. or so, just before dark in summertime. She liked to take her time, looking at any wildlife she might see, and she was sure she saw Bella going across the street into the tall grasses and into the woods that surround a few homes set back from the street.

I told her I'd seen Bella go there many times throughout the years and thanked her for stopping by to tell me. She shared very sincerely that she hoped I'd find her but reminded me that if she didn't come back, "all creatures go to heaven."

The woman's visit had confirmed what my friend Dan had said to me the day before. I had reached out to Dan, an Intuitive and a Tarot Card reader, to see if he could get information about Bella. He had pulled three cards:

1. *Guardian – taking care of you; 2. Growth – a forest card cycle of death and rebirth; and 3. Star – a higher place.*

"Was she sick?" Dan asked.

We really didn't think so, I replied. Yes, she was aging, and we suspected she may have had the beginnings of hyperthyroidism, but she hadn't shown us that anything was really wrong. She may have had a hidden illness, but it was hard to tell, as she was eating and was her normal sweet self.

Dan felt she was protecting us all and had taken control of her situation. She was being a *Guardian* to us. (I hoped the card could have also meant she was protected, being watched over, too) He felt the second card, *Growth* with its themes of forest and cycles of death and rebirth, was telling him that she went into a wooded area (which is what the lady on the bike saw) and that she had passed on. The third card, *Star*, further elicited strong feelings that she had crossed over, and now her star or light was shining brightly. He was so sorry to tell me this in a reading, but he said he didn't feel any trauma associated with her passing. He said the reading felt very clear and grounded but asked me to let him know if he was wrong and she returned.

It was a very helpful reading. There was always food for Bella in a self-feeder on the porch, in addition to her other favorite food she received each day. It would be unlikely that she would just go away from that unless she was sick. Since Dan felt no trauma in the reading, we hope and pray it was her time and she didn't suffer. Since then several kind people have shared stories with me about a cat being sick and going away either to heal themselves or to die. We pray Bella just curled up and let her passing come to be. She had navigated that lake area her whole life so it seems she would know how to take care of herself and wouldn't have become someone's prey.

I trust she is in the light, somehow, and she is free.

My faith in Dan's reading is linked to my trust in him, yes, but I also trust it because it resonates deep within, both for me and for Dale. We can let go and say goodbye to Bella knowing she is free and we are grateful to her for sixteen beautiful years including a parting gift, delivered through Dan, of another chance to trust ourselves. Some people don't like cats because they feel they are too independent or aloof. I have always loved cats because they teach us how to love and trust ourselves. We will always love you, Bella, for being free and going your own way. Thank you for helping me to see the beauty in life, even at its end.

Rosemary Hurwitz, MA. PS.

Rosemary Hurwitz, MA. PS., is passionate about an inner-directed life and she found the focus for it in the Enneagram, a time-honored personality to higher consciousness paradigm used worldwide.

Rosemary has studied and taught the Enneagram since becoming certified in 2001 and is an accredited professional member of the International Enneagram Association. She gives Enneagram-based individual coaching for emotional wellness and deeper Spiritual connection internationally. Rosemary has certifications in Intuitive Counseling and Angel Card Reading and uses these wisdom traditions in her spiritual teaching and coaching. For twenty-five years, along with her husband, Dale, she gave Discovery Weekend retreats, patterned after Marriage Encounter, for Engaged couples.

Rosemary has taught the Enneagram at Common Ground in Chicago for the past ten years and has brought it to Continuing Education in colleges, corporations and on cruise ships as well as holistic centers. She has been published in nine inspirational compilation books, including *No Mistakes: How You Can Change Adversity into Abundance.* Her first single-authored book is the bestselling, *WHO YOU ARE MEANT TO BE: The Enneagram Effect.*

Watch for her online class coming January 2020 on Facebook Live.

Connect at www.spiritdrivenliving.com.

Chapter Five

Best. Cat. Ever.

Mari Cartagenova

Mr Fur. Best. Cat. Ever. Always in our hearts, never forgotten.

*B*est. Cat. Ever. This is what we wrote on your urn. It wasn't an exaggeration. Mr. Fur, you weren't like a cat at all. You were more like a person trapped in a cat's body. When we found you as a tiny kitten on the mean streets of Los Angeles you were just six weeks old and in rough shape. Your eye was all infected, you were covered in fleas and having some tummy troubles. I wasn't looking for a cat, but you came into my life anyway filling a void I didn't know I had. Animals have a way of connecting to us even when we don't think we need them. Without me even asking, you became my savior.

You were adorable. I remember when you were an itty-bitty ball of fur, I would put you in my purse and carry you around to take you out for walks. When people saw your smooshy little face peeking out of my bag, they would smile and laugh. You were such a character. One of your favorite things to do was to go for a ride in the car. I'd say, "Come on, Mr. Fur" and you would actually jump right on my shoulder. Sitting very still, you perched like a gargoyle. Everyone loved to see you planted there, riding around like royalty, showing your magnificence to the world. I still remember the feeling of your soft fuzzy face brushing against my cheek as we zipped up the Pacific Coast Highway. Those memories are what sustain me to this day. You were a wonder cat. And you changed my life fur-ever.

You weren't just a cat, Mr. Fur, you were an angel covered in a fur suit. Your signature move was to sit very close by me and reach out one of your paws so that just the tip of your fur was touching my arm. You wouldn't be on top of me but were always nearby, reaching out reassuringly as if to say, "It's okay, Mom, I'm here." You lived to be twenty-one years old, which is really old for a cat. But I know you would have stayed with us forever if the laws of the universe made that possible. Whenever I was sad or hurt you would come up and snuggle close to give me comfort. You were very intuitive and always seemed to know what we needed. When my daughter was going through her "dressing everything up" stage, you patiently tolerated her putting you in outrageous clothing and even painting your nails! Yes, you were incredibly patient for a cat. I remember a time when you were ill and I stayed up all night sitting vigil by you on the couch. I swore to you that I would always protect you and take care of you. And you looked up at me with those translucent amber eyes that said, "Yes, mom and I'll always be here for you too." And you kept your promise.

There came a point in time when you grew too old and too sick, and I knew you'd be departing the world soon. I'll never forget when I got the call that all pet parents dread. "You need to come down here right now," the vet said. I knew in my soul, Mr. Fur, that you were holding out to be with us. We rushed down to Tufts Animal Hospital and our hearts broke when we saw you in that cage hooked up to a bunch of tubes, your life slowly draining away. I poked my head in the cage and said, "Mr. Fur, Mom's here," and you used all of your remaining energy to lift your tiny head up to look at me. Your gaze was so filled with love and brimming with relief that your family was here to save you. The vet bundled you up on your bed to prepare you for your last car ride. She even gave you a hot water bottle and a floppy crocheted blanket to keep you warm. You looked fragile snuggled up in your makeshift bed, but we had to get back on the freeway to make the long sad journey home.

Of course this was a day where there had to be a lot of traffic. My young children were in the back trying to soothe you while I was jockeying for position on the highway. I was freaking out hoping you didn't die before we got you home. You deserved better than that. We finally made it to the house and put you in the kitchen, which was where we spent most of our time. We kept you warm and me and the children all laid on the hardwood floor, surrounding you. We patted and hugged you for hours, crying the whole time. It was a really heartbreaking – how could we go on without our little earth

46

angel? We knew you had lived to a very old age for a cat but it wasn't enough time for us. Not by a long shot. We had done everything we could for you and now there wasn't much left to do except to say goodbye. How do you say goodbye to a beloved friend? I remember my young daughter cuddling you, petting you and crying. You just looked up at her like the wise old Buddha as if to say, "It's okay, honey. I will always be around all of you. I will never leave." And in those last moments when we were all lying on the hard kitchen floor, stroking your head and telling you it was okay to go, I remember your breathing quickened and I started screaming, "Mr. Fur, Mr. Fur!" Blistering tears streamed from my eyes like a woeful waterfall. And then in one last breath, you were gone. We all huddled together on that joyless kitchen floor and cried and cried and cried. I never thought I'd stop.

You were more than a cat – you were our confidant, our comforter and our friend. We held a celebration of your life that night in our house. Between our tears and sobbing, we wanted to remember you the way you were. The kids drew quirky pictures of you and wrote sweet poems about how much they loved you. My two-year-old said, with tears running down his face, "We wove you, Mr. Fur. Pweese don't go!" Everyone broke down. We all slept next to your body that night because we just couldn't let you go. When the time came to pick out your urn I chose the most dignified and elegant one they had because that was you. It was a burnished amber color with flecks of green just like your ethereal eyes. You were regal and strong until the end. And under your name on the urn, all it said was "Best. Cat. Ever." And you are.

I still remember that night after your crossing. I was exhausted from the crying and the grief. When I went up to my bedroom to try and get a wee bit of rest, much to my shock, I saw your fully materialized Spirit there. You were walking around like you were healthy and whole. I knew you had come to say goodbye and to let me know that you were okay. Hot tears began spilling from my eyes and burning down my cheeks. My sobs echoing throughout the house. I was so grateful for your visitation and to be able to see you and say goodbye one last time. I will never forget how even in your passing, you came and comforted me. That is a gift I will treasure forever. Thank you, my angel, Mr. Fur.

***

Some people say because I'm a medium and an animal communicator that I'm more able than most to connect to animals. This may be true, but I grieve like everyone else and have had a very hard time recovering from the loss of Mr. Fur. I'm not sure I've ever really "recovered." I have, however, been able to use this experience to help my clients not only to connect with their animals but also to process their sadness. So many clients over the years have had similar experiences with the loss of their fur babies. I remember one in particular – he was an older gentleman and very stoic, but when he called me for a reading I could feel he was trying to hold back the tears. His beloved cat, Farley, that he had adored for many years, had recently passed away. With his voice shaking, he told me how this tiny animal had taken care of him. As I connected to this kitty energetically he showed me how he used to stand up on his back legs and wrap his paws around this man as if to give his human a hug. The cat showed me how he nuzzled the side of the man's face. As I relayed this information, the client broke down crying and exclaimed, "That's exactly what he used to do!" confirming to me that his kitty was indeed present. Even though my client had certainly experienced other tragedies in his life, losing this small creature that had been so compassionate and loving toward him had left him completely devastated. Animals are here on this earth to be our mirrors, to show us what we need to learn, and to be there to support and comfort us. That's why it is so hard to lose them.

Many people say, "Oh, it's just a cat or a dog," but every animal lover knows that they are so much more than that. They are beings of pure love, and their souls don't know limits like we humans do. In many ways our animals are our greatest teachers and greatest supporters at the same time. I think that is why they touch us so deeply and in intangible ways. They are sparks of the soul looking to go home.

Mr. Fur taught me and my family so many things. He taught us about compassion. He taught us about love. When the kids were bickering he would go up to them and gently put his fuzzy paw on their leg as if to say, "It's okay, guys – let's try and work this out." The kids would laugh and we would all regroup. He taught us about being okay with how things are. When he was sick, he never complained. He was always very noble and brave, even though I knew that he wasn't feeling well. He never wanted to burden us. Animals teach us to always be in the present moment and focused on the good things in life. Mr. Fur was always about love. And he was always giving. Even when he was dying he made sure that we could all be together when he passed because he knew that's what would help us to heal. When Mr. Fur looked up at us for the last time with those giant amber eyes, they almost seemed to flicker with the light of eternity. His eyes were very special as they always seemed to imperceptibly flutter in his head, rolling around like little golden marbles. I knew the wisdom of those eyes would forever be watching over us. Mr. Fur left a paw print on our hearts that could never be forgotten or replaced. As I reach out my hand to barely touch him, I whisper, "I love you, Mr. Fur. You're the Best. Cat. Ever."

Mari Cartagenova

Mari Cartagenova is a Psychic Medium and Animal Communicator serving clients all around the globe. Mari specializes in delivering heartfelt messages from both passed loved ones and living or past pets. She also finds lost and missing animals with the help of Spirit.

When you sit with Mari you can really feel the presence of your loved one. Her connections offer specific details and leave you feeling both at peace and uplifted at the same time. Mari has trained with the top mediums from all over the world, including Tony Stockwell, John Holland, Lisa Williams, James Van Praagh and Lauren Rainbow. Mari is a huge animal lover and lives with her beloved human family, three cats and three horses. She dedicates this chapter to them.

You can contact Mari at her website, MediumMari.com

Chapter Six

Big Ole Boy

Sandra Hanshaw

Bernice, Bullet, and Bob

*M*y first memory of Big Ole Boy (aka "Bob") was of him – all eighteen pounds of long legs and flopping jowls – running toward me from under a huge oak tree on a beautiful September day. Soulful, honey brown eyes peered out from the dark black mask, a long tongue hung lazily out from those velvety folds. I had grown up with big dogs and loved all of them, but I had always dreamed of having a giant – an English Mastiff. This was the first time I was able to pick the breed I wanted and name him/her without having to compromise with someone else. Little did I know that the Universe had been conspiring to bring me and my sweet Bob together for quite some time. Little did I know that he would change my life forever.

My husband Paul and I had just moved to Iowa for our jobs, which required a significant amount of travel. This lifestyle was not exactly conducive to having a dog, but I desperately wanted one and just knew in my heart that it was all going to work out. Paul gave me the typical "we will see answer," which to me meant yes, and the search began. I found many English Mastiff rescues and breeders online; however, there was always an obstacle: the dog had just been adopted, the breeder had decided to keep him, another family was on the way, et cetera. I was losing hope.

Then one, sleepless night, I grabbed my tablet and found a new posting from a breeder an hour away. They had only one blonde boy with a black mask left. One look at the picture and knew I had found my best friend.

First thing the next morning I phoned the owner and confirmed the blonde boy was still available. When I found Paul and told him we were going to look at a dog, he just laughed, shook his head and went to get dressed. A little over an hour later we arrived at the breeder to see an enormous, multicolored male brindle in the front yard, barking and lurching towards us. I started to pull back, thinking this might not be a bright idea, until this blonde puppy with a black mask started galloping towards us sideways. I crouched down to meet him and he jumped into my lap, almost knocking me over and giving kisses. Immediately I knew this was my Big Ole Boy, my Bob. I still chuckle when I recall looking at Paul out of the corner of my eye and seeing him lower his head and shake it. After filling out some paperwork it was official: Bob was part of our family.

Our big floppy-eared boy rode on my lap the whole way home, his tongue lolling as he just looked out the windows, taking it all in. Every now and again he would turn to look at me, cuddling just a little deeper into my arms when he did. There was an immediate connection between us and I knew this puppy was sent to me for a reason.

Five days after bringing Bob home Paul and I were notified that we had to be in Dallas, Texas for work for the next ninety to one-hundred-twenty days. This was the beginning of Bob's post as social ambassador. He adapted to hotel life easily and loved that there was so many new people for him to meet. One of his favorite spots to sit was out by the BBQs on the patio, where everyone would pet him and give him little treats. Bob learned quickly how to ride in the work van and made himself comfortable in the space between the front seats. He liked to watch everything and didn't miss a beat. Over the next three months he quickly grew to seventy-five pounds and by the time we headed home from Dallas he could barely fit in his favorite spot in the van. (To this day he still likes to ride in between the two front seats...or as close as he can get from the back.)

Soon after arriving back in Iowa, Paul and I received a new assignment, one that would allow us to work from home. We wouldn't have to travel anymore! Just as he had done in the hotel, my sweet boy quickly adjusted to his new routine. Bob had to learn how to climb stairs, stay out of the kitchen when we were cooking, and how to get around in the snow. Paul and I had a steeper learning curve: we had to learn how to adapt to the indescribable amount of hair and slobber on the floor, walls, furniture, and our clothes. There was always a trace of Bob with us even when he was nowhere in sight. Eventually, we figured out we had to buy certain kinds of paint to withstand all the wiping down we had to do, and my mom sewed some dog bibs for wiping his mouth slobber. We went through an automatic floor vacuum and two upright vacuums just trying to keep up with the massive amount of blonde dog hair everywhere. We adapted and created a lifestyle for him, rather than him fitting into ours. Bob even took over one of our three bathrooms, and it was not uncommon to find him lying in the doorway, hoping to get a bath.

Bob had ten acres of land to run and play on, but always chose to stick right by my side. He loved to run up and down the one-hundred-fifty-yard driveway, chasing the tractor, checking on the garden or pumpkin patch with me, and helping to feed the chickens. He made it his mission to make sure there were no rabbits, squirrels or other small animals roaming around the property he didn't think should be there. One of his favorite things to do was to watch me mow the yard in the summer. He would follow me for the first few passes then get tired or bored and retire to the porch for sunbathing. In the winter he loved catching snow in his mouth and chasing the snowflakes. I think we both miss that house and the land we had to roam around and be in nature.

Bob has a sense of adventure about him and he has taught me how to reconnect with my inner child. He loves the water and happily jumps into any pool, garden hose sprayer or bathtub he can find. One night I was taking a bubble bath in our garden tub, my eyes closed and my ear buds in. All of the sudden I felt something enormous and heavy land on top of me. When I opened my eyes, there was Bob, all one-hundred-ninety pounds of him, covered in bubbles. There was also water everywhere; bottles sitting on the edge of the tub had gone flying and my glass of wine tipped over.

Bob had the happiest look on his face and all I could do was laugh and feel thankful that he had included me in his antics. (Make no mistake, I quickly learned to close the bathroom door until I heard the click of the lock to avoid the mess in the future; however, I can play back the memory forever and still laugh just as hard now as when it happened.)

One of Bob's favorite things to do was sing, and he was loud and proud when he did it. He joined in every single time he heard "Happy Birthday" and also taught our Frenchie, Bernice, to sing as well. He thought he was a lap dog and insisted on sitting on the couch next to me, and I could not bring myself to refuse him, even after we had to purchase three new couches because he had broken the spine. Bob was also quite a ham and whenever in front of the camera he would immediately cross his front legs and tilt his head to ensure you captured the most flattering angle. But what my sweet boy loved most was to be close to me and give unconditional love and wet slobbery dog kisses. In return I would take him to the drive-thru for a plain hamburger or an ice cream cone, just like my dad had done with his dog Chuck.

We moved from Iowa to Arizona for a few years, which ended up being both a blessing and a curse. The entire house had tile floors and they could get slippery. One day after coming home from work, I noticed Bob was not putting any weight on his back leg and whimpered in pain when we tried to touch it. We immediately got him loaded up and took him to the vet where he was diagnosed with a full tear to his anterior cruciate ligament (ACL). Surgery was the only option. He was operated on the following day and had to stay at the vet's for two days. It was the longest two days of my life; I simply wanted my Big Ole Boy to be okay and be home with me. We are not sure what happened or how Bob hurt his leg, but we assume he slipped on the tile, because he has refused to walk on tile floors to this day. After that, the tile floors became a patchwork of multicolored thick sturdy throw rugs to make sure Bob could get around the house.

Through Bob's rehabilitation we were advised he needed to lose weight, as he had gotten up to a hefty two hundred and six pounds. We also had to do physical therapy with him once the incision closed. We found putting him in the pool was the best option and helped him on his road to recovery. To this day, four years after his surgery, he still thinks he needs to be held around his belly so he can swim in a pool. He has also slimmed down to a svelte one hundred sixty-five pounds, mostly because he only goes to the drive-thru on special occasions now, like his birthday. Thankfully, his other knee did not tear as the veterinarian had predicted. The recovery time from his surgery strengthened my bond with him even more. I realized I would never know what happened and even if I did, I was not able to change it. Bob reminded me to live in the present and focus my love and attention there.

My sweet sensitive Bob has had many names over the years and has learned to respond to them all, including Bob-a-Rino, Bobinski, Bobbie and his favorite, Bobbles. When he gets into mischief, we refer to him as Robert. He hangs his head as he walks over to his orthopedic bed and puts himself in time out. After a few minutes of begging for forgiveness with his droopy eyes, he slowly starts creeping his way back over to me. Once he is able to get his head firmly in my lap, he runs his jowls over my arm to let me know he is sorry. I gently stroke the soft blonde fur on his head to let him know it is okay and call him Bobbles. Immediately his eyes light up and he knows he has been forgiven and wants to leap into my lap to give sloppy kisses to me.

Bob is an old soul and his heart is full of love and compassion for all beings. He first learned how to adapt to life with our cat, Jackson, and then became the good will ambassador to each new addition to our family, Bullet and Bernice. He has helped potty-train both of the new additions and quickly intervenes in any drama between the two. It is not unusual for us to find Bob with all of his siblings sitting around him. Jackson and Bob have a secret love affair and we often find the two of them cuddled up licking each other when they think we are not watching. Bob has created a special bond with each of his siblings and there is such a deep love between them all.

His face has gone from the dark black mask to a face and muzzle full of gray. His honey brown eyes droop a little more, but they still express every thought and feeling he has. It takes him a bit longer these days to get up and he has lost some of the zip in his step; however, he has never lost his sense of adventure or love of playing "light." My sweet Bobbles continues to teach me how to release the past and live every day to its fullest. The Universe brought him to me when I needed these lessons the most, and I can never do enough to show my Big Ole Boy my appreciation for all he has done in my life.

Sandra "Sandy" Hanshaw

Sandra "Sandy" Hanshaw is an Intuitive Transformational Coach; Intuitive Energy Therapist; Integrative Healing Arts Practitioner; and founder of Raise the Vibe, LLC and the Mobile Mystic. She is passionate about assisting others to find their purpose and truth through education and self-discovery, while using her unique combination of humor and intuitive, compassionate and practical guidance.

Sandy is a graduate of the Southwest Institute of Healing Arts. She has over 20 certifications, including Usui Reiki Master/ Teacher, Transpersonal Life Coach, Angel Intuitive Guidance, Mindfulness Guided Imagery and Meditation Facilitator, and Certified Belief Clearing Practitioner. She offers her gifts as an intuitive to clear energy and empower clients to find the best version of themselves.

Sandy enjoys traveling to new places to meet new people and satisfy her need for adventure. She lives in Ruskin, Florida with her husband and fur babies.

Contact:

raisethevibe@yahoo.com

www.raisethevibe.us

www.facebook.com/Raisethevibe1

Chapter Seven

Buddy ~ Teacher, Protector, and Forever Friend

Dena Hanson

Love you, Buddy, always and forever!!

I have had many beautiful pets through my life, and though I loved all of them, I didn't realize until the last few years the many ways in which they have contributed to making my life abundant. They have been my teachers, counselors, confidants and best friends who brought joy to me even during the most challenging circumstances. Indeed, pets are God's gift to us, little angels through which we experience unconditional love on this earth.

Each dog I have had was special in his or her own way, yet they shared many commonalities too. Like Bailey, the furry hero of the movie, *A Dog's Journey*, they all came to me at the time and season when I needed them the most. They also taught me lessons, some joyous, some painful, though, like most life lessons, I didn't always know in the moment what I was meant to learn. For example, I could not understand why each dog had left me when I was not at home. Why hadn't they waited until I had a chance to say goodbye before going over the Rainbow Bridge? It would be a particularly special dog, Buddy, who finally helped me to see the bigger picture.

Buddy, a beautiful black and white Border Collie, came into my life at a time when I was convinced I would never get another dog. I had recently lost another dog, Duke, and it left me with such a feeling of emptiness I vowed I would not go through that pain again. Fortunately for me, God and the Universe thought differently.

Buddy belonged to the parents of a friend of mine, who were elderly and had to move off their farm and into an apartment in town. This meant they were unable to keep Buddy, as Border Collies are working and herding dogs that need more physical exercise than other breeds. Though it broke their hearts to part with him, they knew he would not be happy confined to an apartment. His mama, with whom Buddy shared an amazing connection, was not about to give him to just anyone. She wanted him to go to a home where he would be loved and taken care of. I believe she passed that connection onto me, for which I will be eternally grateful.

Despite my earlier trepidations Buddy quickly became my best friend, my cuddle boy. He was so soft, and it felt so healing whenever I wrapped my arms around him to give him a hug. I learned he loved to chase rabbits and that his favorite treat was Chicken McNuggets from McDonalds, and he learned everything there was to know about me and loved it all with no judgment.

Buddy was a natural protector, and each day, morning and night, he walked around our home to make sure no predators were lurking around to hurt us. (I still feel him doing this every time I look out the window.) Whenever I walked along our trails he was always by my side, keeping me safe, and he was my partner on every project in the yard. Even when I mowed lawn, he would come and check on me every few minutes to make sure I was alright. Buddy was with us for seven amazing years, during which he showered my life with blessings and taught me so many things. Little did I know he would teach me even more after he left his physical body.

I will never forget that day in February 2017 when I left for Arizona to visit my parents. I knew it was going to be the last time I would be able to hold and hug Buddy, tell him I loved him. As I was leaving the driveway he gave me that look – *Goodbye, Mom, I love you!* I really hoped he would still be there when I returned but I knew down deep it wasn't going to happen.

The night before he passed my best friend Facetimed me from my house so I could talk to him. I had to let him know it was alright for him to go. It was one of the hardest things I've ever had to say, but I knew he was suffering and it was time for him to go. As I told him I loved him and said my final goodbye, I realized something: Buddy was protecting me from seeing him pass, just like all my other dogs had. They had not been abandoning me, they had been trying to spare me pain! This time it was if I was right there with him, and though it was agonizing I was also filled with gratitude that I could share this moment with him.

The following summer it was tough for me to even go outside, knowing Buddy was not there to go on walks and be in the yard with me. At the time I wasn't sure what was wrong with me. I now know I had to face the fear of being alone and feeling unsafe. I realized how much Buddy's passing had affected me when my parents came to visit. Usually they helped with the household projects and my husband and I had even some planned for them. But when I mentioned that one of my dreams was to build a labyrinth in my yard, they offered to help. It was like it was meant to be. I know Buddy had orchestrated the whole thing.

I could feel Buddy's presence the whole time we were building the labyrinth, from the planning stages to the moment we laid the last rock. He was with us as my parents and I walked toward the center, and he was right in the middle of the group hug when we got there. It was a beautiful feeling to have him help me heal from the loss of him, plus I got to see my parents in a new light and they finally saw me as my authentic self. I named the labyrinth "Buddy's Path" in honor of this wise and loving teacher and companion.

Since then I have been open to signs Buddy sends me, if I have a question or just need to know he is with me. Ravens, feathers and butterflies are among his favorite things to send, and oftentimes when someone new comes to walk the labyrinth a raven will fly around and let out some noise to make sure I am listening. I know it is Buddy, sending me a message of love and letting me know he is right there with me all the time.

When Buddy passed, I once again said I would never get another dog. But Buddy knew better; he even knew when it was time to bring us together. Two years later, he led me to a rummage sale at the Humane Society. I really did go for the sale but thought, *Okay, I will look at the dogs.* Still, I had no plans to get one. Though I would love to save every dog, I actually have a long list of criteria before I choose one. I also get that special feeling one gets when they know an animal is meant for them. That day, I looked at all the dogs and didn't get that feeling... until I got to the last one. Her name was Lucy, and she was a two-year-old Saint Bernard, born the same year Buddy passed away. Before I knew it, I was asking to take her for a walk and she was so loveable and wanted a tummy rub right away. I asked all my questions on my list about her, including did she like kids, other dogs, cats, et cetera, and they answered yes to all of them. When they added that she loved ranger rides, I knew that Buddy had brought me to Lucy, that she was meant to be part of our family. This is confirmed every time we on one of those ranger rides and I see a black and white butterfly flying right beside us. I know it's Buddy, saying, *Hi, Mom, I am still with you.*

Pets are our family and I am so grateful they love us for who we are and never leave us, so long as we are open to receive the signs. Thank you, Buddy, for joining me on this amazing healing journey called Life! I love you!

If you are missing a pet or a loved one, close your eyes, put your hand on your heart and imagine them sitting right next to you. Tell them what you need to say and *feel* it. Know they are listening, and ask them to send you a sign. Then watch, listen and be open to when they show up. It will put a smile on your face every time. Blessings and Unconditional love to you!

Dena Hanson

Dena is a Reiki Master; Access Bars Practitioner; Ordained Minister; Mind, Body Spirit Practitioner; Labyrinth-builder and teacher committed to helping people heal and to see the light inside of themselves. Through her work, Dena creates a safe place, non-judgmental space where people are free to release physical and mental pain and peel back and heal the many layers of their personal journey. She is forever grateful to the animals who have touched her life, especially Buddy, whose love and spirit inspired her to build her first labyrinth and remains with her in everyday life.

Dena is the author of *Healing Path Journal* and a contributor to the anthology, *52 Weeks of Gratitude.*

You can contact Dena at Accessbars123@gmail.com

Chapter Eight

It All Started With the Mice

Jodie Harvala

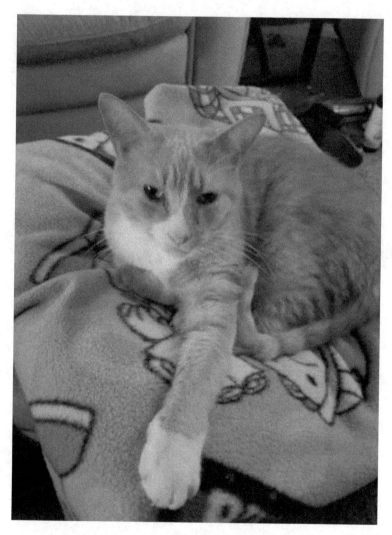

Charlie

"*C*aught one!" my husband would yell out each time I heard the trap go off.

We had never had mice before. Now, to my horror, they were climbing all over my silverware and scurrying across my kitchen floor. They were GROSS, and I could not handle it. Nope, not a mouse girl in any way.

"Caught another one!" my husband exclaimed again, then added, "If you have one mouse you have nine."

That was it. I told him I was leaving until he took care of the mice. (A little dramatic, yes, but that's how strongly I felt about not living with mice). I packed up my older son, Foster (I left the younger one with my husband since he could go to daycare), and we got into the car, destination Minneapolis. My sisters-in-law lived in the Twin Cities and it was the weekend of my niece's birthday party. Perfect. Off we went.

My relatives laughed when I told them why I had taken this mini trip. "Why don't you just get a cat?" they asked. Sounded like a good idea to me. I had always wanted to get a cat but my husband was not a fan. In fact, he'd always told me if I came home with a cat he would re-gift it to someone else so I just didn't bother. My sisters-in-law had a different perspective: they felt *I* had the power in the house and if I wanted a cat, I should get a cat. Their attitude was infectious, and before too long I had decided that yes, we were getting a cat, especially after I heard he had caught six more mice. UGH.

We searched everywhere. We went to every shelter and met all sorts of beautiful kitties. I brought my older son on each outing, for I kept hearing from Spirit that he would be the one to tell me which cat was the right fit. I needed to see a certain reaction from him. This was a very interesting message, for Foster was not a very reactionary kid.

We tried everywhere we could think of and nothing was matching up. My son liked all of the cats but I knew none of them was "the one." A little sad and disappointed, we headed home for a snack and that's when I *heard* to take him to the pet store. We were tired by that point and I wasn't sure I wanted to bother but I kept getting that hit to go.

Let's try one more spot, Foster!

Summoning our last ounce of hope, we walked into the store and headed toward the little white cages housing the felines. And suddenly, there he was. Charlie. A big ole orange kitty just waiting for a scratch. The woman told us Charlie was a great cat and loved to play, then asked if we wanted to get a closer look. I had been hoping for a kitten but as I looked at Charlie I decided to keep our options open. I told the woman yes.

She took Charlie from the cage and led us to a separate room. When Foster grabbed his feather stick and started to move it around, Charlie POUNCED on that thing so fast. Foster let out the biggest laugh I had ever heard! He kept laughing in delight, and I knew this was the reaction Spirit had told me to look out for.

"Well," I said to the woman, "I think we found our new cat."

Then Charlie ran off into the store and we spent the next hour chasing him. Foster loved every minute of it. He was so excited.

I kept asking the woman how long Charlie had been at the store, but she avoided the question. I did find out that although he was a big boy he was less than a year old – still a kitten and quite a silly one at that. He was also healthy and fixed and had had all his shots. He was ready to be with a family, she told me, and we agreed, I would pick him up the next day. I asked her a couple more times how long they'd had Charlie but she would change the subject or simply walk away.

When I returned to the store the following day I did some shopping for our new family member, then went to sign the papers.

Suddenly I stopped and said, "I am not signing this until you tell me how long you have had him."

She turned her eyes down and said, "Nine months. He is our longest stay we have ever had and we just can't figure out why. He has had a couple adoptions, but they return him and we just don't get it. He is the best cat."

I got tears in my eyes and said, "Well I know why. He was waiting for us."

Tears showed up in her eyes too and though I think my words surprised her she knew it was the truth.

I made sure to get Charlie home about an hour before the kids so he could explore a bit in peace, but he stepped out of his box and simply laid on the floor. It was like I could hear him say, "FINALLY I am home." He put his head down and rested until the kids came in the door. He didn't look around; he didn't go hide; he didn't do anything except wait for the kids. Then he followed them around the rest of the day as they showed him his new digs. Charlie was clearly special, though I didn't realize how special until he started helping me in my work as a psychic and space-clearer.

I was very excited when a woman called and asked me to clear her home. It was an old house and it had been on the market for over a year. When I walked into the home the smell of cat pee was overwhelming! I asked if they had owned cats and she said, no, to her knowledge, nobody in the history of the house had cats, and she knew a lot about the past owners. Yet the smell was so strong and made my eyes water.

The basement was the worst. It was not a finished basement, just cement walls and with no furnishings. I walked all over, looking for evidence of cat pee or a stray cat, but found no spots or stains, nothing.

But that wasn't the strangest part. Earlier, I was driving to the clearing when suddenly Charlie jumped out from the back seat and scared the hell out of me! I told Charlie he couldn't come along, then drove back around the block and dropped him off at home. He had never done anything like that before, but I quickly forgot about his odd behavior and focused on the work ahead.

Now, as I was clearing that basement, I had the thought that Charlie needed to help on this one. After all, he often sat in my office when I worked with clients, and I believed he helped with the energy clearing; he had just never come to a jobsite before!

When I left I asked the woman to give me a day to work and we would chat the following day. When I got home I called Charlie into my meditation and sure enough a big black cat showed up. He started peeing all over the walls and when I tried to approach him he hissed and spit and was NOT interested in working with me. Charlie walked over to him and started to work with him. Now to me it just looked like two cats standing next to each other. It was so very strange but in this line of work *strange* is *normal*.

Sure enough, after a few minutes with Charlie the big black spirit cat left the building. Then Charlie got to work on the walls, clearing them of the pee and residue that we all could smell in the physical world. He even turned and looked at me and said, "You can go now, I will take care of this!"

The next day I spoke with my client and told her about the strange interaction with my cat.

"Holy cow!" she exclaimed, "I need to tell you the house barely has any smell in it at all!"

We agreed to meet the next day so I could see for myself.

By the time I got there – forty-eight hours after I had begun the clearing – the entire house smelled fresh and lovely, with not an ounce of cat pee smell in the place! Two weeks later, the house sold.

This experience taught me something very important. Our animals do so much more than we give them credit for. I always knew Charlie was a lover and showed up when our emotions were high. I never, knew, however, that he was an actual light worker!

When my cats come near me and want attention, I stop whatever I am doing and take a few minutes to be still with them. Often I sense afterwards that I needed a break that I was not willing to take on my own, so they forced the issue. My little kitty Ruby does this often when I am working away in my She Shed. She will stand at the door, insisting she come in, then she takes at least ten minutes to calm down enough to settle in for a nap. She walks all over the desks and puts her head under my hands and demands to be pet. She purrs and I breathe. It took me months to figure out what she was doing.

When I have a tough client, Charlie shows up at the door. Most often it's when someone is grieving the death of a loved one. He brings a comfort to my clients that they didn't even know they needed until he rubs up against them and starts meowing his message.

When my little Ruby was missing it wasn't the Facebook posts or hundreds of people I had looking for her that brought her home. It was prayers, of course, but also a hit I got from my guides. A friend told me to keep reaching out to her energetically, to run a pink ribbon from my heart to hers so she could follow it home. Many people also told me that she was turned around.

On the third night Ruby was missing, I woke up and was told to imagine a huge bright light coming up from the house into the sky. I was also to call to her. First I imagined that big strong pink ribbon between our hearts, then I put that light up from the house as bright as I could. I called to Ruby and told her to look for the light! I then fell back to sleep.

Two hours later I was awakened again, this time by a text from my husband, who had fallen asleep on the couch. The text read, "Look who's home!" and beneath it was a picture of Ruby, drinking out of his cup of water. I ran down to check her out and make sure she wasn't hurt and I swear I heard her say, "Thanks for the light!" She was hungry and tired, but otherwise unhurt. I know that light is what brought her home.

Energy and animals go hand in hand; my cats have shown me this a hundred times over as I watch them grow and help my little family through the ups and downs of life. I can't imagine living without them, but I know even when that time comes another sweet animal guide will make its way to us, just as they did. Until that day, I will stop and breathe and pet my kitties anytime they want.

Jodie Harvala

Jodie is a forward-thinking, spirit-loving, space-clearing psychic teacher and coach. She is also the founder of The Spirit School, where she teaches others how to connect with Spirit and how to experience Spirit in the sacred, everyday moments of life. Jodie teaches through experience, using the same tools she developed during her own journey from a "fear-based" woman to a Spiritually FearLESS entrepreneur. Jodie's students leave each class with a stronger connection to Spirit and a fresh perspective regarding the next step of their personal journey here on earth.

Walking with Spirit each day has opened so many doors and brought opportunities and experiences for which Jodie is deeply grateful. The best reward, however, is grabbing another person's hand and saying, "Come along for the ride, my friend! Let me show you the first step!"

Chapter Nine

Jasper: The Barn Cat That Wasn't

Marilynn Wrigley

Jasper

"I'm not really a cat person," I told Jason, the contractor working on my burgeoning bed and breakfast. Owning a B&B had begun as a dream while I worked overseas, and in the years before I retired I had started collecting antiques, trying to complete the picture in my mind – a picture that was finally coming true.

I had no idea the challenges I would face. This day, it was what to do about the "critters" living in the century-old barn at the back of my property. Families had stored their belonging in that barn since 1919, and I had neither the funds nor the strength to clear it. Besides, who knew what treasures it might hold?

"A barn means critters," Jason drawled. "Get a good ole' barn cat, gal. That's the answer."

Jason was my only friend in this new town, a combination of protective older brother and younger, annoying one. I trusted him implicitly, and so I added "Get a cat" to my to-do list, right after "Buy ingredients for hummingbird muffins" and "Pick up artwork for the new cottage."

The day dawned beautifully, and my mood matched as I quickly checked the first two items off my list. It never occurred to me that the old Texan saying, "If you don't like the weather, wait a minute" also works in reverse.

As I drove down the rutted road to the local animal control shelter, a thunderstorm exploded. I parked and ran to the nondescript building door. There was no sign, so I tapped.

"Come in already," came a gruff shout from inside, "and push hard 'cause that danged door sticks like Gorilla Glue."

A moment later I stood dripping on the concrete floor of a room with two metal desks, multiple file cabinets, a live trap, several bags of dog food, and a very large lady dressed in a pearl snap shirt with the sleeves cut out and skintight jodhpurs. Tall rubber boots, caked in mud, completed the ensemble.

"Can I help ya?"

I just looked at her, slightly overwhelmed by the smell of bleach mixed with urine and the sounds of barking in the background. Maybe this was a mistake. Maybe I should just put out a few more traps.

"Well, speak up, sister," she shouted over the barking. "You here to drop off some poor animal you can't deal with anymore because your grandmother died, you live in an apartment that doesn't allow animals, and you have a deadly allergy, or what?"

I was shocked and more than a little offended. I stood primly at her desk and said, "Actually I am here to rescue one of the animals."

The woman looked at me for a moment, then handed me a pen and an application form.

"Sorry, hon. All day I take these poor creatures and put them in cages and watch their 'owners', if you want to call 'em that, walk away without a backward glance. Makes me pretty cynical I guess."

My attitude softened too as I saw the woman's kind eyes staring out from a leathered, wrinkly face. I knew I would never have the heart to do her job.

"I'm hoping to find a barn cat. You see I have a bed and breakfast with an old barn and –"

Before I could finish, she jumped up. "Come right this way – whatchurname?"

"Marilynn. Marilynn Wrigley and –"

"I'm Barbara, and you are in some kinda great luck today, Marilynn Wrigley."

We passed through the door into a room full of barking dogs. She opened another door to a room filled with cats and kittens.

Some were roaming free, playing with toys or draped on a cat tree. I had to admit that the kittens were adorable. Three little ones – a grey tabby with white paws, a tiny ginger, and a black and white tuxedo – were wrestling on a pillow. I was just warming to the idea of having a cat when Barbara stopped in front of a cage inhabited by a huge, sleeping gray cat. His coat was dense and the color of concrete. His head was immense and so was his tail – in fact, everything about him was large. He opened one golden eye and stared at me, then stood and arched his back in a deep stretch before leisurely stepping out of the cage.

"If you need a barn cat," said Barbara with a grand sweeping gesture. "Jasper here is your man!"

I glanced back at the beautiful kittens and wondered if I couldn't just take one of them and teach them to catch rats. Probably not.

"Well, okay if you think he is what I need...?"

Barbara must have noted my skepticism because she began to sing Jasper's praises as an expert critter-catcher. He had ended up in the shelter after his previous owner suffered a stroke and went to live in a nursing home.

I didn't have a carrier, so Barbara found a cardboard crate and laid his blanket in it. She then opened the crate's top and Jasper stepped right inside.

So well trained! I thought naively. *Maybe Jasper is a good choice after all.*

I left with Jasper's intake file under my arm and a cat in a very heavy cardboard box bumping against my leg with every step. On the drive home, panic set in. I had remembered to buy cat food, but what else would I need? How could I make sure he stayed in the barn? What if he ran away, or got in a fight with that prissy Persian

I had seen sunbathing on her front porch and her owner sued me? The doubts about the cat seemed to mirror the doubts I had about my ability to turn my dream into a profitable reality.

At home, I took Jasper into the house to give him food and water before relocating him to the barn. He hopped out, ignored my offering and strolled around the house. He smelled everywhere and curiously rubbed against all the furniture and door facings. (I later learned he was marking the house as his own, so this should tell you a little about how this story is going to end).

I considered picking him up and carrying him outside but was worried he might scratch or bite.

"Come on, Jasper, come on boy," I said, like one does to coax a dog.

Jasper ignored me and continued to explore the house.

"Noooo, no you can't go in the public rooms, Jasper," I said, blocking the doorway. Jasper slid through my legs and continued his exploration. Then I remembered the treats I had bought. At the sound of the bag opening, Jasper jumped onto the kitchen counter, meowing loudly.

"No, no Jasper, you can't get on the counters," I cried. "Oh, my heavens, what have I done?"

I timidly reached under his stomach, lifted him off the counter and waited to be mauled. Jasper just hung there. I slipped my hand under his haunches, and he placed his front legs over my shoulder and rested his massive head. Then I heard it. A low rumbling sound. The decibels increased until the sound was like a small biplane. I'm not sure what happened at that moment, but I think it was the beginning of cat love.

I just stood with my arms around this big, gray animal, then walked slowly onto the front porch and sat on the swing. As I began to rock, I felt large paws push rhythmically against me, kneading.

Another cat lesson learned. Jasper was "making biscuits," the sign of a very contented feline.

I finally took him outside. He immediately ran after a squirrel and jumped from the tree onto the cottage roof. He stood at the peak, crying balefully and staring at me as if to say, "Do something!" I ran to the garage and found a ladder that didn't reach the roof. There I was, sixty years old and with an artificial hip! Was I really going to crawl on the roof to rescue a cat? I looked up at him, calling and cajoling. He just cried louder.

I hurried into the house and called the fire department. Extreme, I know, but remember I had never owned a cat before. When I rushed back outside, I tripped over Jasper who was sitting on the back steps, delicately bathing his nether region. I redialed the fire department, and with a great deal of apologizing cancelled the call, then said a silent prayer of thanks that my neighbors would never know about this fiasco.

"Jasper, get out in that barn and go to work," I said. I think I even stomped my foot. He stared up at me and meowed loudly, so I ran to bring his water and food bowls, thinking perhaps he had gotten dehydrated from his ordeal. The training had begun – my training, that is.

That night I agonized about leaving Jasper outside. I dressed for bed and tried to watch television, but often turned down the volume to listen for sounds from the barn. I stood on the back porch, peering into the dark. Nothing. I tried to convince myself that Jasper was hard at work.

I returned to bed, but a few minutes later my eyes popped open. What if he found some of the poison I had put out for the rats? My heart began to race.

After several minutes of tossing and turning, I again put on my robe and slippers, grabbed a flashlight, and made my way to the barn.

When I opened the barn door, Jasper streaked out into the dark. I called out to him but heard nothing. *Foolish old woman,* I thought, and felt tears forming. I was beginning to find my lifelong dream very stressful. I was beginning to doubt everything.

Sadly, I made my way back to the house. The back door stood open. I stopped in the kitchen just long enough to grab a large bag of M&Ms – my drug of choice. How could I expect to be a successful innkeeper if I couldn't even keep a cat for more than a day?

I walked into my bedroom to find Jasper curled on my favorite pillow, eyes closed, purring loudly. Relieved, I sat on the edge of the bed and petted his dense fur. Not wanting to disturb him, I crawled to the other side of the bed and put my second favorite pillow under my head. I was almost asleep when I felt his soft toe beans rest on my cheek.

The next day I advertised a barn sale in the local paper. I used the proceeds from the sale to have my neighbor's field mowed, after which the rats seemed to disappear overnight. I was out $250 for the cat and supplies and $300 labor for clearing the barn, but I had gained so much more.

Now that his critter-catching services were no longer needed, Jasper became the mascot of the bed and breakfast. He was featured, sitting on the porch swing, on its website and advertisements. Guests clamored to meet him, and he patiently posed as they photographed him dangling from their arms. Each night we shared my favorite pillow, and every night I said a prayer of thanks for Jasper, "the man" who came to live with me.

He has been gone many years, but he brought companionship, laughter and love to my home. I learned that there is absolutely nothing like a warm, purring cat body next to yours. If you are married the story might be different for you, but for a long-single lady, Jasper was as good as a husband, maybe even better.

When I lost Jasper, I found it hard to even consider adopting another cat. The pain was too deep. But I also missed having a companion, and something that felt like a paw kept nudging me. My beautiful Spoiled Sam became my next rescue, and the first time he touched my face with his paw, I felt Jasper next to me.

Marilynn Wrigley

Marilynn Wrigley's thirty-year-career with one of the world's largest oil field supply companies took her around the world and involved dozens of moves – from a tiny thatched cottage in the south of England to a marble palace in North Africa. After retiring, she opened Wrigley House Bed and Breakfast, rated Number One in Brenham, Texas by TripAdvisor for over three years.

She eventually sold Wrigley House and became an inspector for the Texas Bed and Breakfast Association where she helped develop Quality Assurance Standards used in all B&B evaluations.

Marilynn is also a Home Marketing Specialist and owner of Wrigley Redesign and Home Staging LLC; she has served her community on their Main Street initiative and manages two buildings in Brenham. Throughout her careers, Marilynn has kept a journal chronicling her experiences. She shares her home with two rescue cats, Spoiled Sam and Little Girl, who provide diversion during those "writer's block" moments.

Chapter Ten

Jewel. A Diary of Presence

Katherine Glass

Jewel

*J*ewel came into our lives at the perfect time. Our older son Josh had been asking (actually, begging) for a dog for some time, and when he turned thirteen we decided he was ready for the responsibility. I hadn't had a dog since I was five, and though life with my husband Jonathan, our two sons, and our Tonkinese cat Shanti was quite full, I found myself looking forward to having a canine presence in the house.

We headed to the breeder that day intending to choose a dog, but the reality is that she chose us. All of the other eight-week-old adorable, rambunctious puppies were chewing our feet and wriggling all over the place, while the little girl with the hot pink collar ("Miss Hot Pink," the breeder called her) was just sitting there calmly looking up at me. I gently lifted her into my lap, then she looked right into my eyes and sniffed and licked my hands. The bond was sealed.

Jewel quickly became the sweetest, gentlest most playful and loving member of our family. She was also something of an activities director, and got us all outdoors hiking and swimming. She taught us patience, taught the boys responsibility and, most importantly, she taught us about unconditional love and presence in the moment.

When she was eight years old, I began to notice a subtle but persistent fear that Jewel would die. I tried to dismiss it as needless worry, telling myself that I was feeling this way because I knew she was getting older and that Golden Retrievers have an average life span of ten to twelve years; I also believed it because of my history of loss and grief, which is extensive. When I was six years old, my sister died from Hong Kong flu. She was seventeen. My best friend from junior high was killed when she was sixteen. In 2011, my brother passed, followed three months later by my mother and my father a year after that. We lost my father-in-law in 2013, and the next year a dear friend and old flame from my youth passed as well. Indeed, by midlife I had endured more than my share of loss and grief. Now I felt as though I was about to lose Jewel as well.

I even talked to my vet about Jewel's impending departure, to which he replied "Nah, she's only eight and healthy! She's got a long while yet."

Yet my feeling continued, and though I am a professional psychic and medium, it didn't occur to me that I was actually receiving information or a premonition about Jewel's health. I just thought it was plain old out-of-control worry.

When we walked she would stop over and over again to eat grass. *All dogs eat grass,* I thought, *It's good for her.* Then came the thought, *What if she has cancer? Stomach cancer or something? No,* I would say, trying to get a grip, *she's okay.*

I noticed too that Jewel was acting especially affectionate and more needy of my closeness than usual. This went on for quite a few months between her eighth and ninth year, and I kept wondering if she was trying to tell me something.

Then, on November 12 of her ninth year, Jewel stood stock still with her tail tucked between her legs and just looked at me. I immediately called the vet and brought her in. She greeted all the doctors and techs as she always did, with tail wagging, even though she was now in pain. After a thorough examination and some tests, the vet gave us the awful news: Jewel had cancer throughout her lungs and torso. It was hemangiosarcoma, a cancer of the vessels throughout her body. We could put her down right then, or keep her comfortable for about six weeks or so until her passing.

Despite my worry over the previous months, I was in complete shock. Frozen. Everything felt like a far-off echo. I was floating away. How can this be happening? My dog isn't a cancer dog; my dog, my precious amazing Jewel CAN'T BE THIS SICK! She means so much to so many people! All the folks she insists on greeting in the neighborhood, all of our friends and family. Her life can't possibly be over yet!

I thought back to all the times we were walking and I was fearing the worst. I had always told myself, "No, Jewel is protected. Jewel is different, special. She's too young. She's healthy. That isn't our path." Well, actually, it *was* our path, and here we were, right smack in the middle of it. The first of many of Jewel's lessons for me: You are not exempt.

Jewel was given an amazing Chinese herb called Yunnan Baiyao to stop the internal bleeding she was having, which was causing her to feel so terrible and to lose her appetite. We brought her home and within hours she wanted her food and was perking up again. We were so relieved to see her acting more like herself; however, this also made it even harder to accept that we had such a short time left with her. The roller coaster and the lesson of being in the moment had begun. This was also to be the most intensive learning period of resilience, inner strength, and surrender – physically, emotionally and spiritually – that I have ever been through in my fifty-five years. This was, for me, beyond the pain and stress of the losses I had experienced thus far, and even the journey of having two children!

I stayed at Jewel's side through the following eight weeks, with all their ups and downs of emotion and exhaustion based on how she was behaving. When she was feeling well she reverted right back to her doggy ways – sitting out in the rain, chewing her bone, going for short walks, and other things dogs generally enjoy doing. She would go outside in our beautiful backyard and sit very still and calm, looking out into the trees, seeming to contemplate her time left here. She was so present to whatever was going on in each moment. Note to self: Be present! Be calm. I knew that she was guiding me, showing me how not to fear life, death, and loss. Yes, she was dying, but aren't we all? This realization was intensified as it was con-densed into this agonizing period of "impending doom," but the lesson was there, nevertheless. Actually, when I was present with the moment, present to whatever was happening with Jewel and to my tears, my fear, my love for her, my grief, and my joy in her being, I was okay. Jewel so lovingly and gently guided me into awareness of the preciousness in each breath. When she came up to my chair and rested her head looking straight into my eyes with hers, deep, warm and wise, she reminded me to appreciate every gift, every person I loved, every moment I shared not only with her, but with my world, my life, from seeing clients and making coffee to resting on my comfy bed. The little things. Jewel held my heart and taught me about the beauty of simply being.

She stayed with us through that Christmas, for which I was so very relieved and grateful, especially as Josh was able to be with her for the last time. It was a bittersweet, sacred and intense time of preciousness and presence in the moments we were all cherishing. We also kept a close eye on her comfort level and hired a veterinarian hospice expert who helped us watch Jewel and decide when, if necessary, to euthanize her. This piece was always in the mix of our dance with Jewel day to day. We would watch for signs of distress and pain, then give her medications as needed to keep her comfortable throughout these last weeks.

At around six in the evening on January 12, Jewel came and laid down on a large soft mat we had placed on the floor, large enough for all of us to lie with her on. She had never before lain on it without us directing her to, but now she solemnly positioned herself perfectly to one edge, leaving room for myself and Jon to lie with her. She remained there, as if to tell us "it's time" and we dimmed the lights and tearfully and lovingly tended to her comfort level until her passing at two-thirty the next morning. Jewel taught us how to let go of life and accept – perhaps even embrace – death.

It was during her transition, about half-past midnight, that an amazing synchronicity happened. I slipped into the next room and saw that a television special called *The Secret Life of Dogs* was on. It was absolutely no accident that this came on at this time, while

Jewel was leaving us. She wanted us to know her side of the story, of what it was like being in our family, what it was like for her to be our dog. Jewel was magical like that. Her favorite activity was greeting people and giving them what I referred to as her "blessing." When I walked her, if we were passing someone – be it a neighbor or postal worker or repairman, she would lay down and refuse to get up until I allowed her to go and greet them and give them her love. That love came back to her when she was ill and people from all over the world, including sacred places in India, were praying for her. Jewel even touched the hearts of non-dog-lovers. Jewel did that. She melted hearts and brought out the best in people.

We were blessed that aside from a bit of labored breathing in her last hours, she gracefully passed with ease and was conscious almost to the very end. Just as she had in life, Jewel had walked us through the sacred death process with grace and love.

As the sun rose and I gazed out on her domain, our beautiful backyard, I was flooded with gratitude for having Jewel with us for those nine and a half years, and despite the grieving I would go through without her physically by our side, I was grateful that she was now one of our angels in heaven.

January 22, 2019

This morning I had a real visit with my Jewel. I was in the kitchen making tea and suddenly felt strongly compelled to turn around to the spot where she used to stand and watch me. And there she was! Energetically I could feel her presence and in my mind's eye I could see her clearly. She was young, healthy and energetic, with a shiny coat. And she was happy, so happy, that I could see her! It was so vivid that I knelt down and talked to her and acknowledged her presence. We were face-to-face, nose-to-nose, snuggling and kissing like we used to. I felt the curve of her proud chest as I stroked it and she was wagging her tail with the same exuberance she'd had her whole life. I was laughing like there were champagne bubbles in my heart, full of joy at how healthy and happy she was. I felt a little weepy too, but they were not tears of grief but of gratitude that she had come to visit.

I believe Jewel wants me and all of you who read this to know that life is a gift, and that the love you give and receive is precious. Greet every stranger with the desire to lift their day with a smile or a kindness. Treasure the moment, be patient, and don't fear feeling and giving love to your people and animals. Yes, they will leave someday. Nothing in this world is permanent, but that is not a reason to withhold your loving heart. The secret is, that's where JOY resides!

My beautiful girl Jewel. My sweet companion, my beloved Golden Retriever, loved by so many and gone too soon. Jewel walked me through my greatest fear, my dread of loss, like a gentle angel holding my heart through each day, each step, each moment till the end.

Jewel has taught me and is preparing me (even as I write this memoir) for my next journey of the heart. She is reminding me to be brave in the love I feel for the next dog who will come into our family. This is, I believe, a pet's purpose. To teach fearless love, and fearless letting go, and to love even still, and again, and again, and again.

Katherine Glass

Katherine Glass is an award-winning psychic, medium, energy healer and author. She is listed in Jennifer Diamond's *The 50 Top Mediums in the US* (2016) and was named Psychic of the Year in 2013 and 2019 by Best American Psychics. In her private practice in Concord, Massachusetts she specializes in spirit communication, psychic intuitive readings and energy healing.

Katherine has been using her gifts to bring help and healing to others for over 25 years. She is a graduate of the Barbara Brennan School of Healing and Sharon Turner's Awakenings Clairvoyant Program, and has trained at the Arthur Findlay College in Stanstead, England. Psychic intuitive readings and mediumistic readings are given in person, by telephone and on Skype. Katherine is the co-founder of the Healing Essence Center in Concord and hosts the television series *6TH Sense and Beyond: Opening the Spiritual World to the World,* which is available on YouTube. This is her third multi-author publication, the others being *111 Morning Meditations* and *365 Days Of Angel Prayers*, both by Sunny Dawn Johnston. She lives in Concord with her husband Jonathan, their son Robin and their cat Shanti.

Chapter Eleven

My Spirit Horse

Janice Story

Winston

I t was the last night of an incredible weekend in Sedona when I awoke at two-twenty-two a.m., covered in chills, from one of the most amazing, most vivid dreams of my life. I had been hiking in Boynton Canyon and there he was! Running freely against the backdrop of the beautiful red rock canyon walls. Winston had found a way to come visit me. His spirit was so strong that I could hear the sound of his hooves hitting the ground as he came towards me, softly nickering. I could feel his breath when he ran up to me and put his head on my shoulder. Even now, fully awake, I could still feel the presence and love of this amazing animal I'd had such a strong connection with. Not wanting to forget the dream, I grabbed my drawing tools and spent a few hours sketching out the scene so I could capture this amazing experience and easily return to it at any time.

I will always remember the day my husband Kent surprised me with Winston – a reddish/ brown and white paint horse, just like the one I had dreamed of having when I was a little girl. He appeared so calm and gentle as he stepped out of the horse trailer, and I just couldn't wait to get on him. I didn't even get my saddle or bridle; I just hopped on him bareback, looping the lead rope through his halter to use as makeshift reins Not exactly the safest or smartest thing to do with a horse you don't know, but I just felt that he was safe, and of course I was right. In fact, Winston would turn out to be a horse I could let anybody ride, knowing he would always take care of them, and he did.

Winston was my closest confidant; I would sit and talk with him for hours and he always listened. He was never too busy and he never offered advice I didn't want. He just listened and offered me his unconditional love. Horses are great at that! He could always tell when I was upset or hurting, and he would lean his head against me, as if to say, "I am here, it's okay." When things in my own life were tough or not going well, I was always drawn to spend time with the horses. Now that I do equine therapy with my clients and see firsthand the incredible healing powers of these creatures, I know why. Indeed, when in 2010 I was on the scene of a horrific accident that spiraled me into PTSD, no one seemed to understand what I was going through except Winston. His patience and unconditional love were instrumental in my healing.

Over the years Winston had developed arthritis in his knees, which along with being navicular (meaning inflammation or degeneration of the navicular bone in the hoof) caused him to become lame. Thankfully we were able keep him comfortable for a quite a while with treatment and medication. His condition had continued to deteriorate until I was only able to take him out on short trail rides. After a while, he couldn't even do that, but he still had the desire, so I would just get on him bareback and ride around the barn for a bit. I had known for some time that I would eventually have to make the awful decision, and now that time seemed to be getting closer and closer.

The veterinarian suggested that we put him down on the same day I was called to testify at the trial for that accident. Knowing I was not in the emotional space to make that decision, I told Winston that I needed him to let me know when it was time…that he would have to be the one to tell me when he was finished. About two weeks later, his message to me was very clear, and it was one of the most difficult and heartbreaking days of my life. I felt as if I had truly lost my best friend. I was so fortunate to have been able to share a part of my life with him, and he will always hold a very special place deep within my heart. Winston still comes back often and visits me in my dreams. He truly is my Spirit Horse!

Never Give Up

A few years back I received a phone call from KT "Rusty" Armstrong, a friend and a thoroughbred trainer with whom I had worked on the racetracks in New Mexico. Rusty was reaching out to see if I would like to have the trophy that one of his horses, "Hit Me Now," had won.

"What? Really?" I exclaimed, touched that he remembered how much I had truly loved that horse.

A short time later, I received the trophy – a beautiful hand-crafted Nambe silver platter that had been engraved with a horse and his name – which to this day is proudly displayed on top of my china cabinet.

I first met Hit Me Now (aka Panda) when he was just a yearling. I had recently left a very abusive relationship and was in a very dark place in my life, but I quickly fell in love with this little dark brown (nearly black) horse with an extraordinarily playful personality. He also had an extremely swayed back, earning him the Spanish nickname of "Pando," which somehow ended up as "Panda." Panda was a rather hyperactive horse, and you had to be careful when you put him out on the hot walker or snapped him to the rope, as he would start bucking and squealing and you didn't want to accident- ally get kicked.

When Panda turned two and was ready to race, he had some pretty impressive workouts, and showed a lot of promise to be a great racehorse. Then I arrived at the barn one day to find that he was really sick. The veterinarian came to check him out and delivered the devastating news: Panda had colitis x, a very severe intestinal infection. It causes a sudden onset of profuse watery diarrhea and development of hypovolemic shock. Death may occur within three hours of onset of clinical signs. In less acute cases death occurs within twenty-three to forty-eight hours, but it is almost always fatal.

The biggest challenge with colitis is that because of the diarrhea you cannot get the antibiotics to stay in the horse's system long enough to kill the infection. It is also extremely difficult to get them hydrated or keep their fever down. The veterinarian was coming by every four hours to hang an intravenous bag full of antibiotics, fluids and vitamins on him. I stayed with Panda as much as I could during the day and slept in a lawn chair outside of his stall every night to help keep an eye on him and be available for the vet. Yet even with all our efforts he continued to get weaker every day. Though the situation seemed hopeless, Panda wouldn't give up. I have never witnessed an animal, before or since, who was that sick and just kept fighting to stay alive.

After several days his gums and tongue had started to turn a deep purple color and the vet said he would have to be euthanized to end his suffering. I clearly remember crying and begging Rusty to not let that happen, but it seemed we had done everything that we could. This was thirty years ago and I did not know much about anything holistic. But a friend of my mother's was into that kind of stuff, so I asked Rusty if I could at least call her for advice. At this point, it couldn't hurt anything and we were out of options.

I was surprised when Mom's friend suggested we try regular kitchen black pepper, but I was willing to do anything. Rusty and the veterinarian agreed to give me until the next morning, if Panda even survived through the night. I quickly drove to the nearest grocery store, buying the biggest container of Schilling black pepper that I could find.

Now for the hard part, getting it down his mouth, as pepper doesn't exactly mix with water very well. I ended up just pouring as much as I could in his mouth and using a large syringe full of water to try and flush it down. I believe I got at least two-thirds of the can into him. We kept up with the antibiotics and fluid routine, and just prayed the he would survive the night. By the next morning, Panda's gums had actually changed color a little and the diarrhea was not as watery. Apparently, pepper stops up the digestive system, thus allowing the fluids and medication to do their work instead of immediately being forcefully pushed out.

Two days later Panda was feeling much better – his bowel movements were back to normal and he was even able to eat and drink! It felt like a miracle! However, though he was gaining his energy back, he was having a hard time walking. Panda had run a fever for so long that he had almost foundered (this is another term for laminitis, a painful inflammation in the tissue near the hoof). The farrier – a person who trims and shoes hooves – came, packed his feet with medicine, and fitted him with special shoes. He would have to wear them for the rest of his career, but that was okay. Hit Me Now made it back to the races, and boy could he run!

I grew to love that little horse so much. I would go into his stall every afternoon and lay down with him to take a nap. I would lean against his shoulder, he would put his nose around to the back of my knees, and we would both fall asleep. Most horses would not let you do that, and certainly not thoroughbred racehorses! Rusty was always afraid that Panda would become startled and accidentally step on me, but I trusted him and knew that whenever he was ready to get up, he would pull up on my pant leg so I knew to get out of his way. I would share my thoughts and the most challenging times of my life with him. I could tell him anything, and he never judged me; he just loved me unconditionally.

He was also a consummate athlete. Hit Me Now gave every race one hundred percent effort. He won many races, including a New Mexico Lineage Day race when he was three years old, for which he was awarded the trophy I mentioned earlier. He was also named the champion three-year-old New Mexico-bred horse of the year, and thirty-plus years later I still proudly wear the belt buckle he earned.

I have been around thousands of horses on the track over the years, and many have touched my life, but Hit Me Now will always be remembered as one of my favorites. He taught me to always remain strong and never give up! You are capable of winning even the toughest races in life! He was a true survivor, and proved himself to rise above and be the best that he could be, despite his challenges. I am not sure if I helped save his life, or if he saved mine, but I have a feeling it was a bit of both!

I have had so many amazing animals during my life it was hard to choose which ones to write about here, and so I would like to at least mention and acknowledge a few of the others. There was Shooter, whose story was written about in another book, as well as Tomma Tale, Smokey, Jolly Scout, Leo, Cannot Be Ignored, and Pasta Fasola, all of whom were special horses. There were also hundreds of amazing racehorses that gave me the most profound feeling of freedom while I rode them on the racetracks. My current horses – Bailey, Cowboy, and Dreamer – are just amazing and are helping me to empower others to change their own lives. There have been some incredible dogs as well – Peewee, Patches, Charlie, Cheyenne and especially Sport will always be in my heart. And I cannot forget my feline companions – BC, Dutchess, Pepper, Ranger, Cowboy and Ariat.

Each taught me many lessons, but none more profound than this: don't be so afraid of loss that you don't let yourself open your heart up to an animal. Though their passing is painful, the love, joy and healing they bring you more than makes up for it.

Janice Story

Janice Story is a certified Reiki master/teacher; mind, body, and spirt practitioner; published author and speaker; and Equine Coach who also brings over thirty years of horsemanship into her work. Janice's compassionate and gentle spirit provides a safe space for others struggling with physical, emotional, and spiritual trauma. She works with a team of seven horses with whom she shares a strong connection and who were instrumental in her own healing. Together, Janice and her equine team create an opening for healing and transformation that far exceeds that of human contact alone. Janice has a beautiful sanctuary at her home where she sees clients and hosts various classes. To find out more about working with Janice, you can connect with her at janice.story@me.com and www.janicestory.com

Chapter Twelve

Our Earth Angels

Georgia Nagel

Shooz & Midnite

How do I choose?

I was looking at black Lab and Golden Retriever puppies that were being given away. For sure I wanted the one with the white front feet and white chest and looked like a black Lab, but I was also drawn to the black, long-haired one that resembled his mom, a Golden Retriever. I asked the owner if I could have two and he said yes; he then told me the long-haired male was spoken for, but a little female was available. I decided against it and told him I would be back when the puppy with the white feet and chest was ready to be picked up. It was Halloween when I returned and saw the long-haired puppy was still there. I commented that the people must not have picked him up yet and he told me they had changed their minds and took the female instead.

I drove away that day with two male puppies, brothers who had never been separated since birth. This should be an adventure, I thought, which was confirmed a few moments later when they both proceeded to throw up in my vehicle. That was how my life with them began and something told me that was how it would end, especially with the long-haired one. I also felt he would not be with me nearly as long as his brother, a feeling I did not like.

I also named them on the drive home – the lab-looking one with the white feet and chest I called Shooz, and his long black-haired brother, Midnite. Eventually I just called them "boys" since they were always together and I was always talking to both.

Our first year together was interesting. Being retrievers, they were mouth-orientated dogs, so lots of things got chewed on or demolished. I observed that Midnite was the protector, always laying between me and a door. It didn't matter if it was a bathroom door, shower door or bedroom door, he was always facing it. Shooz,

I would learn, was my teacher; I just needed to learn how to listen to him. I also realized that these two were different from other dogs. I often felt that they understood what I was saying to them and, sometimes, even what I was thinking. I would soon find out that my hunch was right.

One night I was working on the computer doing bookwork; both dogs, now about two years old, were laying on their beds. I had been working for about an hour when Shooz came up and nudged my elbow with his nose; when he did that, I heard the words "Midnite gone" in my head. I patted Shooz on the head and continued on, but five minutes later he did the same thing, nudged my elbow with his nose and I again heard the words" Midnite gone." I patted him on the head one more time and continued with my work. When Shooz nudged me the third time and I heard the words "Midnite gone," I shut the computer off and turned around to give Shooz and Midnite some attention. That's when I saw that Midnite was not laying on his bed. I have some long, low windows in the house and Shooz walked over to them. Both windows were open and I noticed the screen was missing from one of them. When I walked over there and looked outside, there was Midnite, walking up the driveway! Shooz had told me every time he nudged me that Midnite was gone and I had not paid attention. It would be very different from here on out.

Time flies for everyone but especially for people with dogs; one minute they are puppies and next they are old. When Midnite was nine, the premonition I'd had the day I brought them home as puppies came true. He became very sick and I took him to the vet, leaving Shooz at home. It would be the first time they had ever been separated, but I explained to Shooz what was going on and that we would be back. The vet said Midnite possibly had pancreatitis. They gave me a bunch of pills and told me to boil rice and hamburger to feed him. I brought Midnite home, made the rice and hamburger, but he continued to get sick throughout the night. The next morning, I tried the hamburger and rice mixture again, giving the same to Shooz since they ate in elevated bowls side by side. Shooz ate his food but Midnite did not touch his. I loaded Midnite up and took him to a different vet. They did x-rays and determined that Midnite was full of fluids and his organs were enlarged. I looked in my Midnite's eyes and could see he was ready to go, that what I had felt all those years earlier was coming true. I held him as he crossed over, bawling my eyes out. After a difficult drive home, I walked into the house clutching Midnite's collar to my heart. I sat on Shooz's dog bed with him, holding him and crying. I told him that Midnite was not coming home, that he had gone to heaven. Shooz licked my tears, walked over to Midnite's dog dish and ate his food that was still sitting in the dish. He knew his brother was not coming back.

The next few months were very hard. I would go to buy a dog toy for Shooz and look down and see I had placed two toys in my cart. I had always bought two of everything, as if I had twins, and now one was gone. There were many nights when I dreamed Midnite was sleeping on the bed with me and Shooz, and it was so real I could feel his fur on my face. I truly believe he came to visit often, always my protector.

Shooz and I moved on as best we would, and he truly stepped into the role of teacher. Back when the "boys" were two, I had started a pet sitting business and was around a lot of animals. The silent conversations that Shooz and I had been having all those years were starting to flow over to other people's pets and so the animal communication took hold. This never would have happened without my "boys" and their guidance.

One March day when Shooz was thirteen and a half, we walked back to the river, his favorite place. There was ice on the river, and before I could stop him he walked out onto it and fell through. He was too weak to pull himself out so I walked out onto the ice, grabbed his collar and pulled him to shore. As we lay there, both wet, my arms around him, I suddenly knew he would be with me one more year. I treasured that year, and just as my premonition of Midnite's passing had come true, so too would this one.

One morning the following March, I went to feed Shooz and he couldn't get up. I picked him up and he fell back down. I stood him up again and he could only walk in a circle. He laid back down and when I looked in his eyes, I saw the same look I had seen in Midnite's eyes that awful day. Then I heard the words, "It's time, Mama." I knew Midnite was waiting for his brother, but this didn't make it any easier to let him go. If you want to know the true meaning of "unconditional love," get a pet.

During my twenty-something years in the pet-sitting business, I have met many pets, and they all have their own personalities and quirks. I have seen some amazing animals – blind dogs that can find their way around their homes; a three-legged dog that can run up and down the stairs faster than I can; a dog with one eye that has camped with its owner all over the United States, Canada and Alaska; and a border collie who can dig through a pile of her eighty (yes, eighty!) toys to retrieve the one you asked for. I even taught one of my cat clients how to say "turkey" when he wanted it! I know a horse that helped a young girl through her difficult teenage years, and of dogs and cats that have warned their owners of a fire in their homes. Then of course there are the dogs that help our servicemen and women with PTSD. I have experienced it, seen it and been told countless stories, yet I am always amazed by our pets' abilities.

Since the title of this book is Heaven Sent, I could not finish this chapter without telling you about a white dog named Lily, who belongs to a friend of mine. Lily had been found wandering around a trailer park and sent to a shelter, then rescued from that shelter in the hopes of training her to be a service dog. Two months later, the people realized it would not work; Lily had a heart of gold but was way too active. So Lily found herself back in a shelter, which was where my friend and her family found her. The shelter did not know anything about Lily's breeding, just that she was a mixture. The family decided to do a DNA test to find out. They got the test, swabbed Lily's cheek the next morning, and sent it off. One day my friend got a call from the lab that was doing Lily's DNA; they wanted a picture of her and asked some questions because they thought someone was playing a prank on them. Apparently, they had run computer testing on the swab and when the results did not make sense, they redid the test by hand, with the same puzzling outcome. They explained that the swab was an excellent specimen, but they could not find any breed in their data bank that matched Lily's DNA. Indeed, they told my friend, she had a very unusual dog. I must agree, for when I visit Lily, she exudes a positive loving energy that I can feel deep inside. She cannot get close enough and tries to hug me any way she can. I have often thought about Lily's test and thought, what if Lily is an angel, sent from above and disguised as a dog? Could that be why she has no match to her DNA? Is it possible? Anything is possible if you believe.

At the time of this writing, Lily's owner, whose husband is deployed overseas, told me that the first night he was gone she woke up the next morning to find Lily laying in his spot on the bed. Lily has never, ever, been allowed on the bed, but there she was, watching over my friend and her family while her husband is away. Can our pets be sent to us from above? I believe they are, but Lily just might have a little more "Heavenly Angel" in her than most.

Georgia Nagel

Georgia Nagel is an Animal communicator and Earth warrior, living, breathing and sharing the sacred connectedness between our spirit and the Earth. Her personal journey has been intertwined with animals, nature and earth wisdom. Georgia believes that if we would share the unconditional love from animals and nature and apply it to those we encounter, we would together shine a brighter light upon this world. Everything has a spirit, honor that.

Georgia has authored two books, *Pet Talker: Listening to Those Who Speak Silently* and *Maurice the Goat Finds His Real Family.* She has also written chapters in many compilation books.

To work with Georgia or to find out more information you may contact her at www.georgianagel.com or gnagel@arvig.net.

Chapter Thirteen

Our Four-Legged Guardian Angel

John Newport

Our rescuer, with a perpetual puppy-like persona and a heart of gold.

*J*ack, our precious ten-pound Chihuahua mix, came to us from the shelter serving our beloved city of Tucson. It didn't take long for my wife Ann and I to realize that this "rescue dog" had come into our lives to rescue *us*, bringing us so much closer together and filling our lives with unbridled joy and laughter, combined with an ever-flowing abundance of unconditional love.

I should start with a few words about how Jack came to live with us. I had previously been a cat person, opting for low-maintenance pet ownership. Ann, however, had several dogs growing up and it was obvious that she deeply missed her most recent dog Ginger, a Golden Brown Aussie with the sweetest disposition you could imagine. Sadly, she had passed away several years before we moved to Tucson.

One evening Ann and I were driving to a movie and came across a distraught little dog running around our neighborhood without a collar. We posted a note on the community mailbox, and by the time a frantic young woman came over to pick him up, I was smitten with the idea of having a full-grown little doggie around the house.

Early the following week we drove down to the pound to begin our search. After a frustrating morning checking out countless numbers of dogs, Ann and I were just about to leave when I spotted a little Chihuahua mix in a cage hiding under a much larger dog. The sign on the little dog's cage identified him as "Jack." We took him out to the get-acquainted area and he enthusiastically kept jumping up and licking my beard. I wasn't sure if the beard made him think I was part dog or if he just wanted out of the shelter, but we instantly bonded. The rest, as they say, is history.

During our honeymoon period with Jack, he constantly had us in stitches with his crazy antics, and we were captivated by his extreme sensitivity and perceptiveness. One morning as we were laughing over his latest escapade, I said, "Hey, someone should write a book about this guy!" Ann agreed and I encouraged her to take the project on. She immediately replied, "John, I believe YOU should write that book! You're always pounding out those "save the world" books and opinion pieces – I'd LOVE to see you write a fun book for a change!"

Intrigued by her suggestion, I called Jack into my office to mull this over. Not surprisingly, his vanity won out, and he agreed to the project under one non-negotiable condition – HE would be the senior author and I would assume the role of his obedient assistant. (By his own admission Jack is a manipulator par excellence – that guy definitely has a way of getting what he wants!) We finally settled our dispute with a tug-of-war with one of his toys, and he won, as always. As by that time I was totally hooked on the project and I readily acceded to his terms. And that was how *The World According to Jack: A Dog's-Eye View with Self-Help Advice for Other Dogs* (Transcendent Publishing) was born.

One thing's for sure, you can learn a helluva lot spending months on end sitting behind the keyboard with your dog, getting inside his head and heart. Ann even told me I was beginning to pick up some of his traits. "Now that's taking it a bit too far!" I replied indignantly, then without a second thought excused myself to wander out back and take a pee.

In his recently published opus, Jack treats readers to a dog's-eye view of the world, with commentary ranging from the inhumane environment of the pound to musings regarding his many obsessions, including food (much to his vet's disdain), lizards and ground squirrels. He also insisted on including five chapters "for dogs-only" offering fellow canines his sage advice on "training your human parents."

Upon reflection, it's predictable that I would wind up with an animal as my alter ego. My path in that direction began with the inspiration of two wonderful people who both came into my life a little over thirty years ago. The first is Ann, who continues to teach me the true meaning of love and devotion and introduced me to the wonders of exploring nature and hiking in the wilderness. The second is my dear friend, fellow author, renowned workshop leader and shamanic guru, Dr. Steven Farmer, who inspired me to follow my calling as a writer and also encouraged me to open my spirit to the wonders of nature – particularly through honoring the Native American tradition of communing with animal spirits. I invite you to read either of Steven's books on this fascinating subject, *Power Animals* and *Animal Spirit Guides*.

Since moving to the desert nine years ago I have become increasingly attuned to the spirits of the animals, birds and even plants that I encounter in my morning hikes along the desert trails. I am no longer surprised by the totally unexpected and sudden appearance of an animal or bird whose spirit communicates to me precisely what I need to learn at that moment. My animal guides have included Road Runner, Hummingbird, Wolf, Coyote, Raccoon, Jack Rabbit – and now Chihuahua.

Getting back to Jack, I recently asked Ann to brainstorm with me the special qualities he brings to our lives that will forever leave an enduring paw-print on our hearts.

In short, this little guy is perfect for us. We never cease to be enthralled by his boundless energy and enthusiasm that springs from his perpetual puppy-like nature. He is extremely perceptive and attuned to both of us, especially in terms of bringing us up when we are down. He truly has an uncanny sense of knowing when either of us is feeling tense or sad – and responds by instantly jumping up on our lap, wagging his tail non-stop and covering our faces with doggie-kisses.

I am totally convinced that dogs have been universally endowed by the Creator with a special gift for healing. In particular, dogs residing in a loving home tend to have a profound calming and healing impact on humans by virtue of the unconditional love, warmth and genuine caring they instinctively convey to people, unless they pick up warning signs that someone might pose a threat to either themselves or members of their human pack. I marvel at the mutually symbiotic bond of caring and healing that so often exists between dogs, and other pets, and their humans.

Four months ago, Ann underwent major surgery at a local hospital. She was in the hospital for several weeks and Jack kept my spirits up while I was home in between my daily hospital visits. When she returned home, he maintained a steady vigil by her side throughout the months of her in-home convalescence. As Ann and I are both physically active, it was extremely difficult for her to accept the initial restrictions on her activity. Fortunately, our little guardian angel has kept our spirits up with his non-stop clownish antics and his unlimited supply of unconditional love. His upbeat demeanor has also prompted me to keep up my daily reminders to Ann that she is progressing in her recovery – an invaluable perspective that I, as an observer, am able to provide when she becomes frustrated with these temporary limitations. Indeed, the three of us have now resumed our morning walks and we're taking full advantage of the coolish September mornings by climbing the hills at nearby Catalina State Park. Be sure to check out Catalina Park if you're ever visiting southern Arizona. With its awesome desert scenery including a majestic collection of Saguaro cacti, together with an abundance of dog-friendly trails, that place is truly the eighth wonder of the world!

Ann has also been encouraged and heartened by our daily routine with Jack. When we are sharing an endearing moment, he immediately runs over and looks up into our eyes, clearly wanting to be a part of that very precious moment. Indeed, every tender embrace turns out to be a joyful three-way hug!

He immediately senses when we are going out without him, and though he is obviously saddened, he automatically lies down and patiently waits for us to come back. When we return we are given the red-carpet treatment – accentuated by his dashing all over the house at ninety miles per hour and immediately initiating a three-way round of "catch the toy"!

These are just a few of the spontaneous surprises we are constantly blessed with through his presence. Simply put, that little guy continues to bring so many awe-filled moments into our lives – moments that bring us closer to each other and to this marvelous little creature who miraculously came into our lives. Yes, beyond a doubt little Jack is truly our four-legged guardian angel!

John Newport

John Newport is an eclectic author, speaker, commentator and co-author of *The World According to Jack: A Dog's-Eye View with Self-Help Advice for Other Dogs*. John, who lives with Jack and his wife Ann in Tucson, Arizona, holds a PhD in psychology and according to Jack is "nuttier than a fruitcake." For further information on his latest collaboration with Jack, *The World According to Jack*, available from Amazon, visit Jack's website:

www.jacksworldk9.com

For information concerning all of Dr. Newport's published books, visit his author page on Amazon.

Chapter Fourteen

Rose and Her Six Kittens

Linda A. Mohr

Calico Rose in Camouflage ©2014

"One small cat changes coming home to an empty house to coming home."

~ Pam Brown

*M*y heart flutters as I turn off the highway onto a five-minute stretch of rock road. I wonder how many times I have made this turn. Thousands, probably tens of thousands! I pass over a bridge and meet a white pickup truck. A man waves. I wave back and wonder who that was. But that's what we do in the country. A left turn at the next fork in the road takes me by a house. I carefully navigate through deep ruts without getting stuck. I emerge at the top of the hill, and the next curve is in sight. A jungle of trees and Holstein cattle keep me company as I pass through a low muddy area where the creek has been out for the umpteenth time. As I round the bend, the second bridge comes into view. I smile when I see R. Mohr on the mailbox. According to author, interior designer and contemporary philosopher Alexandra Stoddard, home is a spa for the soul. I can't agree more as I turn into a lane that leads up to my own five-star spa on a hill. I am home.

I honk the horn the traditional three times to alert the dog, Packer, and my mother. She probably won't hear me, but in a minute she will see me. My long day of travel that started at 4 a.m. to catch a flight followed by a four-hour car drive is history. The hassle is worth it just to see my mother's face. Packer's custom is to greet me at the car door. My kindred spirit does not disappoint me. How I adore this brown and white spaniel! I pound on the back door as I open it and call out, "I'm home, Mother."

The kitchen's warmth envelops me. I exhale. A quick scan of the room reveals supper in progress. A white Corning Ware dish with blue cornflowers sits on the counter with a partially assembled tuna noodle casserole. The peas wait in a strainer. Three unopened cans of tuna are stacked nearby. An oven-fresh cobbler, warm and bubbly, cools on a wire rack.

"Blackberry?"

"Yes, your favorite," she says.

I suddenly jerk my head up and glance around the crowded plane cabin. Everyone is sleeping and except for the whirring of the jet engines, all is quiet.

M. Scott Peck opened his book *The Road Less Traveled* with the famous line "Life is difficult." Some days are difficult. Some years are difficult. For me, this is one of those days and years rolled into one great difficulty. I am flying from Florida to Missouri six days before Christmas to prepare the farmhouse for the holidays. I plan to decorate the house, shop for gifts, wrap festive packages, plan a menu, shop for food and bake goodies—a gargantuan undertaking of my own making. My intention is to make the best of an unimaginable year of grief and to transcend the current circumstances, if only for a few hours on Christmas day. My family lost our brother-in-law, mother, first cousin and uncle in a span of eight months. My sister Donna is uncertain if she will come home for Christmas. My brother Larry is a retail manager and works through Christmas Eve. My younger brother Steve works until a few days before Christmas. So it is a one-woman show!

A light snow is powdering the sleeping countryside when I arrive at the farm. Exhaustion overcomes me, and I sit in the car for a couple of minutes, looking at the dark, lifeless house and dreading going inside to nothingness.

Finally, I find the strength to get out and walk over to the garage door. When I open it, I hear an unexpected rustling followed by a meow. An adorable orange, black and white cat appears and greets me as if she has known me forever. This must be the stray Steve, who is looking after our mother's house, had discovered in the garage four days earlier. When he opened the door to the house, the calico followed him inside and jumped on Mother's kitchen chair, a one-of-a-kind solid wood heirloom that the feline could easily use. Steve had bought cat food and checked on her daily. He named her Rose—after our mother Rosemary.

"Well look at you! You are still here."

I unlock the house, and the green-eyed beauty prances in and jumps on Mother's chair again.

The second act is recast, with me now in a supporting role. Her needs become my needs. I waste no time in moving the water and food bowls into the house and freshening them. I am so engrossed in caring for Rose that the pain of not seeing my mother when I opened the door is tamped down. The reality that comfort food is not on the counter does not distress me. What matters now is Rose!

Rose's arrival is intriguing. Cats have not lived on the farm for years. Where had she come from? How did she get in this garage? Why now? I think of my life coach, Sacha, who has emphasized that I do not have to know the how. The Universe is cooking something up. Neighbors are few and far between. Steve asked around, but no one claimed the calico. The cat is skinny, but in remarkable condition for fending on her own in December. Although I do not know *how* the cat found its way, I do know *why* the Mohr house was its destination. Our mother had sent this loving creature to soften our family's sorrow. Shortly before my mother's passing, she told me she could help more from another place. She could be with all of us at the same time, and we would feel her presence. From the instant Rose follows me inside, playful energy flows through the house. An unforgettable Christmas miracle is being orchestrated from above.

Rose knows where she is going to sleep beginning with the first night of my arrival and until my departure ten days later. Where else, but in the middle of my bed! She provides comic relief as the emotionally charged decorating activities unfolded. While I rummage through drawers and closets looking for Mother's favorite decorations, Rose paws around. She follows me from room to room.

She plays hide-and-seek. She seems accustomed to being inside and does not hesitate to jump on furniture. She does not bother the stockings hanging from the fireplace mantle or the fiber optic tree lighting up the guest bedroom. The green ceramic tree my mother made and the ceramic lighted schoolhouse that symbolized her thirty-year teaching career are safe with Rose. The whimsical Snoopy decorations hanging in the bay window do not cause a cat and dog fight.

The highlight of the decorations is the twelve-foot, pre-lit tree adorned with Mother's impressive collection of red and gold ornaments. No bows, no tinsel, just beautiful ornaments and white lights. Rose stakes out a spot under the center front of the tree and delights in snoozing nestled among packages. She will spend countless hours under the tree throughout the holiday. An aura of pure peacefulness surrounds Rose. I sense she is relaying to us a long-distance message:

All is well and all is as it should be. All is in divine order—even sadness.

My siblings and I have a lovely Christmas. I mix our mother's traditions with a couple of new ones. I fill a stocking for each of us with little wrapped gifts from the Dollar Tree store. Some gifts are selected for fun, such as bubble blowing liquid and wand. I get each of us a set of reindeer antlers to wear while we open presents and take photographs. However, the main reason we have a lovely Christmas is because of the spirit of Rose. A research study about women surviving loss and hard times found that strength did not come from enduring the hardships, but from how they survived them and how they sustained close relationships. Donna would later send a note, saying, "We needed to be together and Rose the Christmas cat was the perfect touch."

That Christmas, Rose creates a place where we feel at home. She wears her velvet Christmas ruff so we can photograph her. We help her open packages filled with catnip mice and kitty treats. Her flawless performance helps each one of us to celebrate the "first" Christmas without our loved ones—one of the many firsts we will encounter in the coming year.

Little do we know Rose has more gifts to deliver to us. On June 13 of the following summer she gives birth to six blessed kittens. I had intended to spend a month at the farm to prepare for a fall auction, the daunting, sad task of going through a basement and eight rooms weighing heavily on my mind. However, with the addition of kittens to the agenda, I return to the farm five days after their birth and stay for two months. The babies are tiny, and the tiniest of all has labored breathing for a week. I pray the kitten will survive. Rose and her litter stay under a round table in my bedroom. The table drape touches the floor. Sometimes, I see Rose's tail sticking out. Otherwise, this is a quiet, dark spot for the seven of them. One afternoon I peek under the table and am aghast. Rose and the six little kittens are missing! How can this be! I look through the whole house and eventually find them still in my bedroom, this time well disguised underneath a skirted chair. I realize I have lots to learn about a mother cat and her babies. In this instance, Rose's instinct was to move the kittens to safer area. Maybe I have been looking at them too often!

Once again the energy had changed in the house due to Rose and the six vibrant kittens. I wean the kittens. I play with them and socialize them. I read lots about kittens and am fascinated by what I learn. Rose is supplied with kitty essentials from Larry's store. As the kittens grow, they entertain us and make us laugh. My sister gives them funny names one day, and Steve renames them the next! We take a myriad of photographs. They climb the draperies and dangle from the back of the vacuum sweeper bag. One kitten naps in an antique bean pot; others rearrange the auction items. All of them eventually sleep with me. What a time we have chuckling over their antics one minute and crying over a sweet family memento the next! Rose and the kittens help us survive another "first," and we return to our jobs with the auction preparations done.

Each precious kitten symbolizes new life and hope for the future. The kittens are a piece of Rose, a piece of the family farm, and a piece of my mother Rosemary. When they are twelve weeks old, I select two of the kittens, later named Chauncey and Grace, to fly with me on pet-friendly Southwest Airlines to Florida. Rose and her other babies, now known as Rosebud (the little one survived), Angus, Tigger and Boots stay at the farm and add love and laughter to mother's house, into which Steve eventually moves.

Each cat has enriched my life beyond expression, and I am blessed to spend several weeks a year with them. According to Linda McCartney, if you see something that moves you, and then snap it, you keep a moment. With camera in hand, I capture their distinct personalities for posterity and showcase their moments in time in my annual cat calendar. My mother's legacy of a calico cat named Rose and six little kittens are forever a part of me. Mother could have shopped until eternity and never found a more *purrfect gift* for our animal loving family than this calico cat.

Linda A. Mohr

Linda A. Mohr is an author, educator and entrepreneur. Writing is her "go-to tool" for facing adversity. Her poem "Morning Visitor" received the Cat Writers' 2016 Muse Medallion and won Honorable Mention in the Ageless Authors Anthology. She studied under presidential inaugural poet Richard Blanco at Omega Institute and Mississippi state poet laureate Beth Ann Fennelly at Palm Beach Poetry Festival. Following her Parkinson's diagnosis, Linda created the Parkinson's My Way—Creativity in Motion website and blog in 2018 to educate, give hope and inspire.

Her essays, poetry and photographs have been published in eleven anthologies and nine journals. Linda's memoir *Tatianna—Tales and Teachings of My Feline Friend* won the 2008 Merial Human-Animal Bond Award plus six other honors. She has a master's degree from Purdue University and MBA from Nova-Southeastern University.

Linda is a top-rated vintage eBay seller. She shops thrift stores, teaches strategic management and collects brooches. She lives in Florida with her partner Joe and three feline muses. Vacationing at the family farm is balm for her soul. www.parkinsonsmyway.com

Chapter Fifteen

Ruby

Cher Rue

Ruby

I have had pets all my life, and though I loved them all, some deeply touched my heart and taught me more than I ever could have imagined. My first dog was a German Shepard named Trixy. We were best friends, Trixy and I, hanging out after school and going on hikes and playing with my friends on the weekends. I had her until she was twelve, then one day I came home from school and my parents told me she had gone to "the farm." I didn't understand. I wanted to say goodbye to her and I asked my parents but they said no. I was so sad, it seemed the pain and emptiness would never go away.

After that we had more animals, both cats and dogs, but I never got close to them. The thought of losing another one hurt too much. It wasn't until after I had my own daughter that my heart opened again, this time of one of our cat's kittens. Sammy the Siamese cat was my buddy until he passed from cancer at the age of ten, leaving me devastated once again. After that we just had one cat for years, until my second husband, Jon Rue, told me his dream had always been to get a big dog. Jon, who was ten years younger than me, had fibro-myalgia and was in constant pain. Though I wasn't looking to get a dog, I agreed, hoping it would make him happy.

I remember like it was yesterday the day Jon and I went to get a Labrador puppy, his breed of choice. When we got to the breeder's house, there were about fifteen puppies and fifteen other prospective puppy parents. I turned to Jon and said, "The one that comes to us is the one." We sat on the floor and one came up to Jon and another, a tiny chocolate Lab, came up to me. She was just six weeks old and fit in the palm of my hands. Instantly in love, I exclaimed, "Here she is! She's ours!" We named her Ruby.

From the moment we brought her home, any guardedness I felt about getting close to an animal melted away. Ruby was so sweet, I had no choice but give her my heart. Everyone else loved her too, but she and I had an especially strong connection and, as it turned out, a much stronger bond than she shared with Jon. When Ruby was about four I caught him being abusive with her and that was it, I divorced him. Jon wanted her, but no way, Ruby was mine. Over the years we grew closer and closer; she was both my best friend and baby. She was also my savior.

Ruby was there when I was happy and when I was sad. Just looking into her eyes brought me comfort. Ruby loved my daughter and just being around people. We would go to the park or just out in the backyard where she loved to lay in the sun and bathe in it with a big smile on her face. I would go out to the jacuzzi and she would come out of her doggie door and sniff around the yard and check on me or just hang out.

Ruby also loved the milk bones of various flavors I would give her as an afternoon treat. Each day around four she would sit and wait in her bed, drooling and smiling with excitement. I am very social and always out and about, but no matter where I was I would drive home with a smile, knowing Ruby would be waiting for me and wagging her tail as I came in the house. As she rubbed up against me I could imagine her saying, "Mom, you're home! I am so happy to see you! Now where is my treat?" I know I spoiled her, but she really deserved it. She was such as sweet, good dog, who always listened. I could leave food right next to her and she would not touch it until I said it was okay.

At night, Ruby would cuddle in bed next to me as I watched TV. Actually, she was quite the bed hog, spreading out across the queen-sized mattress and leaving me a sliver on the edge. You fellow dog owners out there totally know what I am saying. It's just the way dogs are wired, they want to be close to their people parents and get the love. What I love most about dogs is they do not judge anyone, nor are they picky about who they are blessed to have as parents; they just want to be a good friend and be loved.

Ruby charmed everyone, including my friends, and when we had overnight guests she would just sleep in the middle of whoever was there. She was not about to give up her spot on the bed, but she would totally share it.

She slept with me until last year, when she could no longer get up on the bed. She had started to have a few medical issues at age thirteen and the vet didn't think she would live longer, but Ruby hung in there past her fourteenth birthday. Then she started getting dementia and pooping in her bed in my room every day. It was tough, but that was my baby. My friends suggested I put her in a different room, but I said no, she would be unhappy, she wanted just to be with me. If you are a fur mom you know what I mean, so I lived with the smell and her constant barking.

The year before I had planned a trip to Europe, thinking she would not be around, but now as the trip approached, Ruby was hanging on but declining. I had lots of talks with her, telling her what a great dog she was and how blessed I was to be her mom. I would lay next to her on the floor and just sing to her. I said goodbye when I left on my trip and told her I loved her and if she wanted to go I would see her when she came back. I had no idea how true these words would turn out to be.

One evening around seven p.m. London time, I was on top of a tour bus when all of a sudden my stomach dropped and Ruby came to me in my head. *Goodbye,* she seemed to be saying to me, *I love you.*

"What's wrong?" my two friends asked when I started crying.

"Ruby is gone," I told them, "She just came to me."

"You don't know that…" they said, trying to comfort me.

"I DO KNOW!"

I tried to call Lee, my roommate, but she didn't answer the phone. Later I found out it was because she was so upset she'd had to put Ruby down.

After leaving London we headed to Ireland, where we went into a beautiful Catholic church. I light a candle for Ruby, for though I had not spoken to Lee yet in my heart I knew she had gone.

I found out the details when I got home from my trip. Ruby had stopped eating when I left; she struggled with her back end and could not get up and was pooping in her bed. She was ready to go. Lee called for someone to put her to sleep at home, which was what I wanted, but they were not available for a week and Ruby was not good. Finally, she called my son-in-law and he came and took Ruby to the vet. She was very nervous, but Lee held her and talked to her, telling her what a great dog she was and how much Mom loved her. She told her to go to Mom...

When Lee told me this I looked at her in amazement. She had said this to Ruby just before noon in Los Angeles, the same time I felt her presence while on the bus on London. It had really happened!

These days, I know the connection between us is still there; we hear the doggie door making noise as if someone has gone through it even when it is closed. I know it is Ruby, and I am so grateful that this amazing dog, friend and baby who blessed my life continues to watch over me. Thank you, God, for giving me this precious gift. .

Blessings,

Cher Rue

Cher Rue

My name is Cher Rue and I currently reside in beautiful Dana Point, California. I am an Actress, Writer and Producer. I had my own talk show online www.thecherrueshow.com. I started out with writing "Dear Cher" and I knew I loved to help others. I constantly connect in helping support various charities. Children's Hospital Los Angeles, animal and homeless shelter charities are dear to my heart. I am an Honorary Board Member at the Natural Ivy Foundation www.naturalivyfoundation.org.

I have always been passionate about seeing others happy and helping others to find their inner self and beauty. It is never too late to make your dreams come true. I am currently the Executive Director of the Miss California Queen of Charity, a local pageant for Plus size ladies.

www.misscaliforniaqueenofcharity.com

Chapter Sixteen

Sam—A Shaman Disguised as a German Shepherd

KC Miller

Sam

*W*e didn't choose Sam.

Our son, Ryan, from the remote sand dunes of Afghanistan, scoured the Internet for the ideal, heroic dog who would be waiting for him when he returned from his deployment. By the time Ryan met his furry confidant, the adorable little puppy he'd chosen had morphed into a gigantic, rambunctious, hairy energetic dog. True to what they say about German Shepherds, Sam and Ryan bonded immediately and exclusively. The two loved to frolic inside and out—occasionally breaking furniture—and always causing Ryan to bust out in roars of laughter. It was true camaraderie from the beginning!

When Ryan was unexpectedly redeployed only three months later, both he and Sam were devastated. Sam grew lethargic at night, and was anxious and destructive during the day. Within a short time, we received a call from Ryan's wife saying there was no way she could keep this heartbroken creature in their small apartment.

We had to make a choice: do we break Ryan's heart by giving his dog away or adopt her ourselves?

Sam moved in with us. Of course, we imagined this to be a temporary adoption, which we did more as a duty than a decision. She ate shoes, dug holes, whined at night for the lost love of her life and shed more hair than you could possibly imagine.

Time marched on. Ryan was wounded and returned from military service to begin an extended period of convalescence. After that, there never seemed to be a good time for him and Sam to be reunited. Ryan began medical school, had children and went on to a demanding residency. In the meantime, Sam's allegiance had eventually transferred from Ryan to my husband and me, despite the fact that I held very strict boundaries against her touching me due to my dog hair phobia.

Sam turned out to be a wonderful companion to our old boxer and both dogs were actually very easy to travel with despite their size and Sam's continual hairy exfoliation. I am an avid hiker and walker, and Sam became my companion when our beloved boxer grew too old to traverse the hills and pathways of my adventures.

Once we moved into our new home located on the side of a mountain with hiking paths in every direction, Sam and I ventured out to greet the dawn almost every day. As time passed, she began sitting near me, getting braver and braver each time. She eventually grew bold enough to put her paw right up against my foot while still honoring my boundaries. She never licked or jumped up on me the way she still did when Ryan came to visit even years after they had parted.

Soon after our move, Sam developed a strange habit of eating the rocks she found in our desert yard. We had no understanding of the volume of rocks she was consuming. We were, however, becoming aware of the arthritis settling in her hips, the cataracts forming in her eyes and her inability to jump into the back of the truck without assistance.

As I became more patient and protective of Sam, a kind of dutiful bond grew. At the same time that my relationship with Sam was growing, my quest to understand Shamanic pathways grew, including my desire to discover my own personal Spirit animal.

One day, Sam put her paw fully on my foot, then proceeded to vomit rocks and bile. She initially hid her head in shame, then she looked fully into my eyes as if to explain that her days were numbered and she would miss me dearly. With deep remorse I admit this was truly the first time I had a full locked-on visual exchange. It was as if my soul was in communication with her soul!

As I helped my husband load her into the back of the truck, I knew without a doubt this was our final farewell. I consciously chose to look into her eyes — we exchanged tears and a deep knowing.

Due to my commitment to teach Shamanic Reiki that day at a local college, I was obligated to leave. At noon, my husband messaged me that Sam had transitioned in his arms due to internal bleeding from the rocks in her belly. Seeing that I was overwhelmed with emotions, a sweet student offered to give me a hands-on Reiki session with the intention to help my grief pass and provide comfort.

The student Practitioner used a feather to guide the grief from my heart toward the heavens. For just a moment, it felt as if I left my body and climbed to one of the beautiful plateaus Sam and I hiked to regularly. As I continued to surrender to the guidance of the Shamanic Reiki Practitioner, the most amazing transformation happened. Without explanation, I felt as if I were seeing through Sam's eyes. There was a rush of freedom, then pure joy. With a big exhalation, I knew Sam was free.

A few weeks later I was preparing to teach yet another Shamanic-related class designed to help students discover their personal Spirit Animal. In a morning meditation, the idea came to me to try to recreate the experience of going into Sam's body and seeing through her eyes. Even after asking permission to enter her body from a trance state, I wasn't given access. Instead the message I felt was that I needed to kneel before her, in my mind, and look into her soulful eyes, awaiting a message. Unable to fully explain the experience, I clearly sensed Sam's message to me: *If you would have only let me, I could've given you so much more!*

My heart trembled and bled with shame when I realized how much I had forfeited. My Spirit Animal, Sam, was inviting me to look at all the ways I hold friendship, companionship and unconditional love at bay.

Once I had received her message, I could easily slip into her animal body during Shamanic meditations and see from her wise, caring canine eyes. The adage "When the student is ready, the teacher will appear" perfectly describes my revelation. Just as I was destined to meet Sam as my teacher, I believe we are all destined to meet particular animals, people and teachers on our wisdom path. My Shamanic path has deepened because of my teacher, Sam, a true Shaman.

(**Important note:** Dogs eat rocks because they have developed a condition known as pica, which is a nutritional deficiency. In Sam's case, we fear that her condition was likely created by changing dog food based on the recommendation of an unqualified pet store employee.)

KC Miller

KC Miller is the Founder of Southwest Institute of Arts Healing, a nationally accredited college, recognized by the US Department of Education, located in Tempe, Arizona. She is a Life Coach, Yoga Teacher, Reiki Master Teacher, Ordained Minister and Shamanic Gateway Dream Coach with a passion for all things metaphysical. She believes *"Everything is something"* and that there are no accidents in who we meet, rather only "Divine Appointments." KC often assists people with discovering their Spirit Guides and Animal Totems.

She is the author of *Toe Reading — Are Your Walking Your Destined Path?;* a regular blog contributor to various publications; and a contributor to three anthologies, including *Heaven Sent, Living Brave — Finishing Strong,* and *Entrepreneurial GRIT.*

Chapter Seventeen

Sassy Mare Companion

Jani McCarty

Peanut Butter

A horse owner's nightmare...

*I*t was a Monday morning when my daughter Hannah called to tell me that Peanut Butter was having trouble. Hannah had been walking her – dragging her, actually – around the paddock for twenty minutes, but my horse of fourteen years just wanted to lay down and roll.

I held my voice steady as I asked Hannah questions, then told her I would call the vet and head out to the ranch, which was thirty minutes away.

I took a quick shower, jumped into my barn clothes, and carefully backed out the driveway. It was a beautiful sunny Colorado morning. As I drove down the highway, I had to remind myself to breathe. I repeatedly expressed gratitude to my Angels and God for carrying us all, for giving us strength and courage, for holding us in the light, and for dispelling our fear.

I took over for Hannah when I got there, walking Peanut Butter, keeping her from going down. When the vet arrived we brought Peanut Butter into her stall so she could be examined and given fluids. After delivering the devastating diagnosis – colic – the vet intravenously administered Banamine, a drug that would help alleviate her pain and stress.

> *Colic is an insidious condition in horses. It can cause great pain and discomfort while affecting the integrity of their gastrointestinal tract. The anatomy of a horse is really not conducive to effective digestion. Digested food leaving the stomach enters the intestine which makes a loop folding back in the opposite direction before continuing on with its coil of sixty feet.*

Colic forces the horses' digestive system to back up; food becomes impacted, the impacted intestine restricts and begins to twist. The blood supply to the intestine becomes cut off, causing that section, or sections, of the intestine to die.

Most common causes of colic are an abrupt change in food, moldy or tainted food, ingesting sand, not enough water consumption, stress or a drastic shift in weather.

Some of the signs of colic are pawing, rolling, bloating, stress, uneasiness, absence of gut sounds, and the loss of interest in food and water.

When colic is caught early there are treatments that can usually relieve the discomfort and support the impaction to move through and pass. Some horses are candidates for colic surgery, though it is invasive, very expensive, and requires lengthy stall recovery. For many horses, however, colic progresses so rapidly that the damage is too great for them to recover.

It took me over an hour to locate someone available with a horse trailer to transport Peanut Butter down the hill to Littleton Equine Medical Center. Though drugged and uncomfortable, my sweet mare willingly followed as I slowly led her to the back of the trailer. After just a hint of hesitation she stepped in. As I closed the trailer door I was consumed with a wretched heaviness.

I knew this was to be Peanut Butter's last ride. I sensed too, she had already said goodbye to Blondie, our other horse, and to the ranch that she loved.

Celebrating my 50th...

Looking back, I realize that not only were Peanut Butter and I destined to meet but that she came into my Life at exactly the right time. It was the months leading up to my fiftieth birthday and I was reflecting, as I do each year, upon my Life to that point. I realized that this milestone actually felt quite significant, so I looked within to see how I wanted to celebrate *me*. I clearly received a message to gift myself with a new horse partner.

Wow, what a bold idea! Being a horse owner is a huge, long-term commitment, both in terms of time and the money it takes to finance their care, training and shelter/board. This is no deterrent, however, for one who knows that there is nothing more sacred, gratifying, and fun than traveling in relationship with a horse.

It was so fitting that my mother accompanied me on my equine search. Mom was raised on an Illinois farm and had always loved horses. She'd also convinced my dad to let me get my first horse, Ginger, when I was twelve. Preliminary online research had led us to videos of some horses, then to the ranch south of Denver where they lived. As Mom and I headed to the ranch, we were both filled with excitement at the prospect of meeting these horses, with their unique movements and personalities, and hopefully to meet the horse meant just for me.

Mom set up camp on the porch of one of the ranch outbuildings. She sat in a rough chair and had her book to keep her company as I paraded back and forth on the various horses I was "trying out."

The two geldings I rode were nice enough, but I was looking for a horse with a fiery yet gentle spirit, a horse who was feisty, fast and ready for adventure, a horse who could make my heart soar!

"What about Peanut Butter?" Mom asked, and something inside me quickened.

Peanut Butter was a five-year-old mare, registered half-Arabian, half-Quarter horse. She was a beautiful chestnut with a gorgeous Arab head and large expressive eyes. I was enchanted by her energy and grace, yet I also felt a bit threatened and small in the shadow of her presence. Mom was convinced she could be the one I was searching for.

I ran my hand down the side of Peanut Butter's leg to ask for her foot so I could pick her hoof. She gave me her foot and at the same time turned her head around to assess me. I worked quietly as I introduced myself, picking her feet, brushing her hair, and combing her mane.

Several times she and I connected, both of us conveying curiosity as well as caution.

The first time I mounted her and sat in the saddle I noticed how slender her barrel was between my legs. I felt her electrified energy pulsing in anticipation underneath me. I felt absolutely exhilarated. She made me feel alive!

Flanked by two horses ridden by ranch hands, Peanut Butter and I rode out over the bridge. As we rounded the ditch bend, I saw the dirt road in front of us rise up to the top of a bluff.

As the three horses trotted in unison at the base of the hill, I suddenly sensed Peanut Butter's anxious impulse to break free and run. I felt a flash of panic, then something incredible happened – I let go! Like a bullet she exploded forward, moving with such grace, power, and speed. Focusing on my breath, I released my resistance. We moved up the hill like a flash leaving the other two riders stunned and their horses in a cloud of dust.

Out in front I relaxed, giving Peanut Butter her head and relinquishing any control I might have had. We moved rhythmically in sync, scaling the top of the bluff with ease.

Somehow, I came back to earth to skillfully rein her in, having her make circles and finally come to a stop. Alone on top of the bluff, Peanut Butter and I stood as one, heaving breaths and snorting.

Eventually she allowed me to move her back down the hill at a pace at which I could recover.

I leaned forward with my hands on her neck and spoke quietly when I asked her if she wanted to come home with me. She clearly responded in a way I could hear. Not only had I chosen Peanut Butter as my new partner, she had chosen me as well.

Lessons from the heart...

As I said earlier, Peanut Butter came into my Life exactly when I needed her. In addition to it being the advent of my fiftieth birthday, it was also the summer before Hannah started eighth grade and an especially tumultuous period as she negotiated her adolescent identity. Though our relationship was still challenging, we found we connected over our love of horses.

Peanut Butter came to teach me important Life lessons about boundaries, myself and relationships. She reflected in her behavior my attitudes and emotions. I often had to shift my perspective to see what I was offering that Peanut Butter was acting out. Many times she reminded me that I was pushing and controlling in asking for what I wanted.

She also emulated my daughter's obstinate creative spirit. Like Hannah, Peanut Butter was so darn smart and clearly independent in choosing how and when to cooperate. She'd argue my decision to cross an old suspended bridge when the ground below was easily traversed. And when it came to crossing water, she'd cleverly maneuver around it or jump it every time.

Peanut Butter's acute hearing and smell were always the first to alert us of something on the trail. Given her head, she could pick through any footing, leading the other horses on the safest route.

Over the years I spent hours grooming Peanut Butter. It was one of our favorite times of sharing.

I would groom every inch of her body, stroking, brushing, detangling her mane and tail. This process somehow smoothed out the messiness of Life and soothed my own needy energy to rush.

In her focused singleness of purpose, I learned to allow myself to just be, soak in the gifts of the present moment, and savor the knowledge of being enough…

I spent several hours this early evening out at the barn with Peanut Butter. There is something so calming, so grounding about grooming her, allowing her to graze on the new spring grass and watching her just be a horse, content, present, massive yet gentle.

This evening was especially reflective for me. Our daughter, Hannah, graduated from college this morning. Her father and I, her Aunt Lynnie, and boyfriend Shaun all joined her to witness and celebrate this great achievement. Both my sister and I cried, missing Mom and Dad, knowing how proud they would have been.

As I finished combing out Peanut Butter's tail and scraping the dried mud off her back legs, I stood upright and leaned into her, placing my arm over the top of her back, feeling her body.

I spoke with my Angels and asked for clarity and creativity; to be accepting and at ease with myself and the rhythm of my Life. Slowly I positioned Peanut Butter along the inside rails of the round pen. Then with the flexibility I've had since I was a kid, I slid my leg over her back and hopped on bareback.

We rode along together for about twenty minutes, leg yielding, spiraling inward one direction, then the other. Together we glided quietly around the pen as deer picked their way through the pasture below and her herd, stood quietly in the early evening dusk.

This is heaven, I thought.

And I heard my mother say, "Yes, it is Jani. It is heaven on Earth."

Life cycles forward...

We moved Peanut Butter and Blondie to our ranch three years ago last August. For Hannah and me, it was the realization of a shared dream of being able to care for our horses at home. Hannah immediately took responsibility for the morning feed, which she did before work, including in winter when she had to brave subzero weather and use a flashlight to navigate the darkness.

Peanut Butter and Blondie settled into their new home and routine, and the four of us were thrilled to be able to ride in the neighborhood and around our property. We made big plans for all the rides we were going to take. And all the while I denied my growing awareness that Peanut Butter was slowing down. It wasn't until that awful Monday morning that I was forced to face the truth.

It's been almost eighteen months since my precious Peanut Butter left this world for a higher path. And though I accept that her physical Life is over I am still able to travel with her in so many ways. Even so, I felt it was important to have a piece of her here in the physical world.

Her ashes rest in a beautiful cherry wood box at home under her saddle stand in the tack room.

Peanut Butter, you have been – and continue to be – my sassy mare companion and my sweet spirited, sensitive friend. I will love you always…

Jani McCarty

Jani McCarty is an author, speaker, entrepreneur, Transformational Life Coach® and Heal Your Life® Coach. Since 2009, Jani has focused on teaching, coaching, and partnering with others in their transformational journeys. She believes by virtue of living, we are given the opportunity to define ourselves, to make our own choices, and to take action that truly determines the direction and quality of our lives.

Jani's genuine interest and compassionate presence have a way of making others feel good about themselves. She generously shares her wisdom gleaned through thirty-five-plus years of her own transformational journey, including her recovery from drug and alcohol addiction, in order to help others remember who they are and reconnect with their path, power, and purpose.

Jani lives in the foothills of Evergreen, CO with her husband Bryan and their dog Charlie. She celebrates Life with family and friends, communing with nature and journeying with the spirit of her horse, Peanut Butter.

www.janimccarty.com

Chapter Eighteen

Sebastion ~ The Story of Us

Jennifer Wheeler

Sebastion

*"Whoever said diamonds are a girl's best friend...
never owned a dog."*

~Unknown

$\mathcal{L}$ ife is about constantly changing and growing. When I met Sebastion I was in a time of great change and growth. He was my teacher, my guide and protector. Most of all, he was my best friend. I've always thought that was so cliché, but as I remember him now I know, maybe it is cliché, but it is also true. It is what he was, and still is for me.

The Story of Us begins on Christmas Eve at the Walmart in Payson. I was going to get batteries for my camera when I saw a cardboard box full of puppies. As I walked up to the box I knew it was probably not the best time to get a dog. I had recently moved to Arizona from the East Coast and was just starting to heal from a tumultuous relationship. I had very little money and absolutely no experience owning a dog, much less raising one from a puppy. The man selling the puppies was unhappy, because his purebred Queensland heeler had gone out on the town and had a torrid love affair (or so I imagine it). Because of this, he was selling the "mutts" for only *twenty dollars*, plus they were just so damn cute!

I went inside to think about it for a while, my head spinning and my heart thumping. On one hand I had no idea how to raise a puppy and it seemed like a big undertaking, on the other hand this was a fresh start for me and I had wanted a puppy for as long as I could remember. Wandering the store in indecision, something suddenly swept over me. I jumped into action, got the batteries, and emerged from the store with a twenty-dollar bill in my hand.

"I'll take the girl," I heard my voice say.

"She's gone," the man replied. I looked down into the box and looking back at me were the sweetest, brownest eyes staring back. He had a blue ribbon around his neck, and his little nose was twitching as if he had known, the moment he smelled me, that I was his person.

I heard my voice again, and this time it said, "Yes. I want him." I saw my hand shove the bill at the man, and then the puppy was in my arms. This tiny puppy was coming with me, up the mountain, to mom's house for Christmas.

Mom greeted me at to door with a grin. "I thought you were getting batteries."

"I did," I replied, "They had puppies too."

Though I was already in love, I also had a fair amount of anxiety about raising a puppy. Was I ready for this? I knew the answer was probably not. I was living in an apartment with my sister and working two jobs just to make ends meet. Fortunately one of my jobs was at a veterinary clinic and I could turn to my coworkers for advice.

When I was a kid I was never allowed to have animals. One time I brought home a puppy from the neighbor's dog. I begged my dad to let me keep it, the answer was still, and always was, no. I was heartbroken. I didn't understand why I couldn't have a puppy, or even a cat. Looking back, I realize that having a little girl and a puppy seemed too much for a single father.

My entire childhood I desperately loved animals and was compelled to touch and love on every animal I could. My dad would say, "Jennifer stop petting every animal you meet, they don't all love you." Ha! I thought, of course they do! I promised myself I would have as many animals as I wanted when I grew up. At 18 I moved out on my own, and the first thing I did was get a kitten.

Shortly after I got Sebastion, my sister and I moved to a house in Tempe, where she started classes at Arizona State University. I became a flight attendant, which was rather ironic because I was a homebody and found traveling kind of intimidating. It was comforting to know that Sebastion would be there when I got home to give me hugs and kisses and of course let me throw the ball for him.

When I was home, Sebastion followed me everywhere, he was my constant companion. Most of the time with a ball or a toy in his mouth. If I didn't throw the ball for him he would nudge my hand with his cold wet nose or strategically place the ball in front of my feet so I would have to kick it as I walked. If I was sitting, he would put the toy in my lap, and if the toy moved at all he would pounce.

He was also a quick learner. I always talked to him like he was a person, sometimes it was about what was on my mind, other times it was instructions, and when I told him to do something he figured out what I meant and did it. We had inside and outside toys, and he knew the outside toys were not to be in the house (they got kind of gross.). All I had to say was, "Sebastion, take that toy outside," or "You know that is an outside toy," and he would take it out the dog door. When I said, "Pick up your toys," he would take them over and drop them in the basket. He was clever, for sure, but it was more than that. We had a special connection, and it was almost as if he could read my mind.

Sebastion and I were growing together. As *he* grew he learned a lot of tricks, but only did the ones he wanted. For a long time he refused to roll over. One day, I caught him hungrily eyeing the hotdog I was eating.

"If you want it," I said, "you have to roll over." I then waved my hand around. He did it! Now I knew he could do it. He still didn't like it, and whenever I asked him, he would whine loudly, then do every other trick he knew to see if that was good enough.

As *I* grew I was healing and learning about who I was. It was a time in my life when I was unsure of the direction I was going. I knew I wanted to allow in more happiness and a new way of thinking. I was improving myself and I was starting to think about the values I held dear. I was forming my own opinions, and letting everything else go.

Part of this healing was my regular visits with Mom. We had had a rocky relationship for many years and we both saw my move to Arizona as an opportunity to start over. Every other weekend Sebastion and I would drive to Strawberry and go with Mom and her dog, Little Bear, to the forest. Sebastion loved these outings as much as I did. He chased anything and everything, even pinecones, he was most definitely a dog of play. Little Bear played the momma, playing with him and gently correcting him when needed.

Mom and I grew really close and we talked almost daily on the phone, she had finally become my best friend. When I picked up the phone Sebastion knew, he would grab the ball, run outside and wait for me to come out. I would sit at a table on one end of the backyard and throw the ball toward the old metal shed at the other end. Sebastian would run and slide into the dirt around the shed, eventually wearing a small hill. The conversations were usually long, so he had plenty of time to play. I cherish those moments with my mom and my dog.

Sebastion was five when my mom was diagnosed with lung cancer. She had opted not to undergo treatment, and by the time she came to live with us she was very sick. I took care of her the best I could, and my sister took over when I had to go on a trip. Every night I was home, I would lay with her for a while and then go to my room, where I would listen to her cough and struggle, knowing there was nothing I could do for her.

I felt like a little kid again, filled with the familiar fear of Mom leaving me. I spent many nights crying and praying she wouldn't die, and that somehow she would heal herself. My work trips were particularly hard; I felt guilty about not being there, and yet at the same time it was a welcome relief to not have to hear her cough, or moan in pain, for just a little while.

I was away the night my sister had to call an ambulance. Mom never came home, she went into hospice where she died four weeks later. My pillow and my dog collected many tears in those months, and I don't know what I would have done without Sebastion. He was there to help me navigate my grief and eventually move into this new chapter of life without my mom.

The very next month I met the man who would be my husband. My whole life all I had wanted was to be loved. But I had spent so many years watching my parents hate each other, and wondering how they were ever together; I had also had my own share of toxic relationships and I was determined I was not going to settle. I had known for years what my ideal partner would be like, so I started to solidify those qualities in my head and even started writing letters to him almost every day. I also talked to Sebastion about him as I wished, hoped, and waited. In the meantime I learned how to be happy alone, and when he did come into my life I had no doubt it was divinely guided.

My husband was amazed by the connection Sebastion and I shared. Sebastion had this way of looking at me when I talked to him. He would tilt his head to one side or the other, give a little whine as if responding, and stare right into my eyes. Oftentimes he knew I was talking to him, even when I wasn't looking his way!

When my sister moved to Georgia we adopted her dog Amber, which was fine with Sebastion because they adored each other. They had very different personalities – Amber was always a bit of a wanderer and Sebastian was a protector. One day they got out, I don't think Amber meant to run away; she was just following her nose. Sebastion went with her, even as she crossed over the highway and eventually wound up in a neighborhood about five miles away.

We were so relieved when we got a call from a lady who had been able to read Amber's name tag. She told us that Sebastion was not interested in coming near her, or letting her near Amber. He just watched warily while his friend approached this strange human.

That was his heart; he loved Amber so much that he was willing to make sure she was safe, even if it meant leaving home. He did the same for me and I always felt safe and loved when he was around.

As the years passed, I could see Sebastion was starting to mellow out, and the red-orange color on his muzzle became peppered with white. Still he remained my constant playmate and companion. He was with me when I was pregnant and snuggled with me through all those days of exhaustion and nausea. When I needed a nap, he slept alongside me. When he started having problems with his hips it became difficult to jump onto the bed and into the car. He was still able to swim, and he loved to dive deep in the water for toys.

Sebastion was there when I went into labor with my daughter, never leaving my side for the six hours until I went to the hospital. He was there when we brought the baby home and in the coming year would show endless patience with her as she climbed on him, hugged him, and eventually ran around with him. Always her mother's daughter, she loved animals as much as I did and she was always giving him hugs and kisses.

As Sebastion's hips gave out on him; he also became paralyzed from his midsection down, probably from a tumor on his spinal cord. For a couple of months we carried him outside with a carrier, and even though he could still use his front legs, he was a ninety pound dog, and this was not an easy task. My husband was gone for work much of the time and I was left to tend to Sebastion by myself, while still taking care of my fifteen-month-old. When I would take Sebastion out, my daughter would stand at the edge of the concrete and scream for me, which is so hard on a new momma heart. I couldn't go to her, because I had him. Oftentimes my heart was torn between these two precious beings who needed my attention. But somehow I managed, even taking him for acupuncture appointments and making sure he spent some time in the front yard each day.

One day I looked into Sebastion's beautiful eyes and for the first time saw sadness in them. I realized that this amazing dog who had been my faithful friend for the last fourteen years was ready to go. I was not ready to let him go, but I knew it was best for him. The night before we said our goodbyes we took him for a walk in the wagon. One last time around the block, one last time all of us together. Aside from losing my mother, it was one of the hardest moments of my life.

Sebastion taught me patience and unconditional love, because he gave it to me. He guided me through some of the hardest and some of the happiest times in my life, because he was always my companion. I always felt safe with him, which allowed me the space to heal and become myself. He truly helped me change and grow.

After Sebastion died I missed him terribly. I was overcome with joy when I was able to connect to him through meditation. It started out simply. I imagined a forest with a clearing and I saw him there happy, young, and playing again, still helping me on my journey. At first I had to search him out while meditating, but as time went on, he started coming to me on his own. Now, I know he is there. There are times I feel him stronger than others, but he is always with me. I still feel his love. I am grateful for the difference he made in my life and the friendship he brought me.

"When I come into your dreams, I'm really there.

When you see me out of the corner of your eye,
I'm really there.

When you 'sense' me around the place, I'm really there.

I haven't left you, not really.

My spirit is everywhere but especially with you."

~Unknown

Jennifer Wheeler

Jennifer Wheeler is a Certified Life Coach, Reiki Master, Intuitive Angel Guide, and author. She finds joy in being with her loving husband, watching their amazing daughter grow, and having all the fur babies she wants. She finds much enjoyment traveling with her family, as well as being home and basking in the warmth of the Arizona sun.

Jennifer loves combining creativity and her intuitive gifts to help others. She finds inspiration in the magical side of life and is passionate about allowing children to nurture their gifts, imagination, and, most importantly, the belief that anything is possible.

Connect with Jennifer

Flowerjen76@gmail.com

Chapter Nineteen

Taylor Made

Raina Irene

Taylor, Nov 28, 2006-Sept 22, 2019

*T*aylor was two years old when she entered my life. Grafted in by marriage. She had just given birth to eight black puppies. The question always remained: who was the father to these half yellow Labrador pups? We would never find out. Yet each one was the dark version of their mother. But mother she wasn't. She was a puppy herself.

"Do I have to nurse them?" she would question us as she laid there, doing what she instinctively knew was her calling of the moment, while yearning for her daddy, Richard, my husband, to please throw the ball. But she did her due diligence, hoping one of these tiny babies would want to play also. One by one the puppies flew the coup and Taylor pranced in relief that this season was over, and she could get back to "puppying."

About a year into our grafted relationship, I was disrupted with frozen shoulder, an unbearable issue without question. You truly cannot move your arms. Your shoulder is locked in place and if it is nudged, it will send you into a mental breakdown of piercing pain. Taylor, our ambitious pup, was insistent on our attention. Since my arms were locked, my hands were easy access for her nose to remind me she was present. It wasn't long before we had to redefine our relationship and I had to remain inside from the nose-prodding. I could only hang out with her through the screen of our sliding glass door that divided us. My heart pain was as intense as my shoulders that insisted, I keep them still. My solution: a friend. Taylor was an only dog at that time, the only play time she had was when the grandkids came over, or weekends with Rich, because of his long work hours. She needed a best friend.

I love how ideas manifest possibilities. Within a few days, I heard through a friend that a young mother with four large German

Shepherd dogs, was in dire need of placing these animals in homes that would love them. I contacted her immediately and told her to bring them over. I knew I could only take one of them, so the agreement was, whoever Taylor fell in love with could stay.

She pulled up to the house with the dogs packed in her small blue Toyota Civic. As I looked into the window and laid eyes on *Beau,* I instinctively knew it was him. But I proceeded with our agreement. Beau was the second dog to be introduced to Taylor, and the last. She was smitten and so was he. With that, Beau, the mellowest German Shepherd I had ever met, was grafted in. The two of them were joined at the hip. The yard was happy. And I was happy. My compromised body watched the two dogs play and find joy.

I was beginning to unlock at the shoulder while Beau was beginning to appear tired; his hair was falling out and he stopped eating. Taylor would sit by his side; she knew something was off and her time with him was short. We were only allowed one year with Beau before his body would fail him and Taylor and I would realign once more. It was a painful animal year. Within a few weeks our mischievous silver kitty, Raven, would escape our home to find a new clan also. The yard was quiet again. My ninety-five-year-old mother's life was coming to a close. Our lives were changing rapidly, but the one thing that was consistent, was this beautiful dog in the backyard that refused to grow old.

As my shoulders started to move again, my time with Taylor changed also. I could go into the backyard and find solace. I could lay my hands on her, give her love, and Reiki. Little did I realize she was becoming my own Reiki practitioner.

After my mom went to Spirit, Rich and I moved to a larger property and proceeded to fill it with kittens, chickens and mini horses. Taylor ran around the captivating property visiting each one of her new friends with her healing magic. The horses calmed, the chickens were, well chickens. They entertained her. Hurting any of them, or anything for that matter, was nowhere in her doggy nature.

The backyard also provided a pool that became Taylor's personal recreation. This girl could swim like one of the kids. She did laps around us. She would swim all over the pool climbing out from the deep end. She loved playing with the kids but was just as happy to play in the pool with only Rich. He would throw the ball in the basket, she would retrieve the ball, bring it back to him and then back in the pool she would go.

One day I was outside visiting with my lifelong friend Jeanette. Jeanette was processing a situation in her life through our conversation. Taylor came up and prodded in true Taylor fashion. Back and forth she would nudge us, we would pet her, she would leave and then come back. But today was different. Taylor was about to show me something I had not seen before. She came back once more and nested herself in-between Jeanette's legs. This was unusual because, as I said, Taylor was a busy dog. Staying still was not her forte. I paused from our conversation and watched as Taylor made her presence known to us in a way that was unique to her character. I watched motionless. Speechless! What was happening here?

Taylor looked at me and began to tell me what she was doing. There were no barks, moans or movement. It was in her eyes. She was giving Jeanette Reiki! I let out a huge breath that I didn't realize I was holding and said, "Jeanette! Taylor is giving you Reiki!"

Jeanette looked at me, surprised, and then touched the top of Taylor's head, acknowledging, "Oh my goodness, I think you are right. I can feel it!"

We both remained quiet for what felt like ten or so minutes that Taylor stayed still, and then she was off to her next adventure. I was mesmerized by what I had just witnessed. All those moments I had touched her had created a Reiki Master in my own backyard.

Jeanette was the first, but she certainly was not the last. Every person that encountered this loving animal would sense something that would touch their soul. I knew what she was doing every time.

As much as Taylor believed she was a puppy, her body was aging. She could rule the backyard, the pool and the animal kingdom we had created. Regrettably, aging was one thing she could not reign over. None of us can. Her ball-throwing days began to decrease; it was too taxing on her. She had to pick between swimming or a ballgame. Swimming always won. We must redefine all our relationships as we age. Taylor was no exception. We hid the balls. She looked at us, eagerly waiting for the invisible balls until she realized the balls were not coming. But that didn't stop her. With eleven grandchildren, balls were going to be flying through the backyard and into the pool. And Taylor was determined to get them. Swimming was her passion. Though she could no longer leap out from the deep end, she was not going to show us her weaker side. Especially the kids. She was going to give them all the love and Reiki they needed.

Richard and I could tell she was slowing down. The days that followed swimming with the kids were tiring. She struggled to greet us at the door. This beautiful creature's eyes told us a story as we would sit with her on the couch.

"I can't get up," she would speak in a moaning kind of chatter.

"I know, Taylor. You don't have to get up, just stay here, I will sit with you girl. It's okay," we would tell her. Then, two days later, puppy Taylor would be back at the door, waving her tail as if she was two years old again. She would cause us to pause about her health and her age. We would count backwards in years, just to double check our numbers. Then the kids would come over, back in the pool she would go and then once again, she would repeat her cycle. *The old woman in her and the little girl doing the dance of aging.*

A few days prior to her leaving us, Richard called me outside, concerned. She had once again just laid down after swimming, a ritual she was unwilling to omit. She laid tired and slightly untouchable. He showed me some new evidence on her skin that indicated her immunity was failing. It was a Friday, late afternoon. We talked over what we should do next. Richard went back and forth in his mind about what we should do. But we agreed *she* would let us know. The weekend was spent with us both talking separately to our friends about our concerns, as if we knew what we knew, but couldn't speak it to each other.

Sunday morning felt normal. She was out and about and "puppying." We had a full day of out and about ourselves. We left the house for several hours to accomplish our feats. Arriving home around five o'clock that evening. The house felt still. Richard was leaving the next morning to go camping. He had things to do in the front yard, so I set out to the backyard to tend to the animals. The backyard was still also. There was no sign of Taylor at the door and no Taylor on the couch. Where was she? Taylor was not a runaway kind of dog, but ironically, she had gotten out of the yard just a few weeks prior. She had made a new dog and owner friend just around the corner and had enjoyed their pool. Had she seen them walking and wanted to go play again? I began searching. I headed down to the barn, went in and out of the stalls, looked under the trailer, near the fruit trees and in the bushes; no Taylor. I headed back up toward the house to make my way to the opposite side of the yard. As I was about to head down the other side, I heard Rich in the front yard.

"Richard!" I yelled, "I can't find Taylor; she is nowhere back here!"

He immediately dropped what he was doing and followed me down the other side of our yard; *her yard*. We didn't have to take more than twenty steps before we saw her laying in the golden brush that camouflaged her. Down the embankment Richard slid, swift and without caution to get to her. I followed. *She was telling us,* just like we knew she would. Her body was no longer a puppy. *Her puppy mind had been taken over by the beautiful grandmother she didn't even know she was.* Our Taylor, Tae-Tae, Taylor-Made girl was going home.

Taylor gave Richard thirteen years of her life. She gave me eleven. And when I say gave, I mean *gave.* She was a gift wrapped up in creamy yellow fur, our honey dipped girl that endlessly reminded us to always play. "Life is too short. Play with me for just a little while and I promise, you will forget the pain that this life can also *gift* you with."

Life *had* almost crushed me in the last two years, but Taylor would not allow me to slip too far; she was our healer in the backyard and Taylor-Made for us...

Thank you, Taylor, for the prodding of my hand, Reiki and for making sure I knew...

You were always *present.*

Raina Irene

Raina Irene is a Heart, Soul, Spirit Practitioner and the owner of Beauty, Strength & Healing Inc. She holds multiple certificates in Holistic Health, Spiritual Work, Emotional Healing and is a licensed Esthetician.

Raina's Eclectic and Spiritual diversity enables her to tap into your unique needs, supporting and guiding you to clarity and connecting you with your own healing energies. She blends her esthetics with intuition; councils one on one; holds healing circles with the emphasis on inner wisdom and understanding grief. She shares from a heart of experience.

With two Siblings, Parents and now Son in Spirit, Raina has devoted herself to sharing that our bonds continue, and Love is forever...

All you have to do is Believe and you will see.

Friend Raina at: https://www.facebook.com/GypsyRaina.Irene

Like her page at: https://www.facebook.com/gypsyraina

Join her group at:
https://www.facebook.com/groups/BeautyStrengthHealing

And if you have a child in Spirit or would like to share with a friend who does, please join her group:
https://www.facebook.com/groups/lullabyletters

Chapter Twenty

The Bud Man

Debbie Schmitz

Buddy Before and Buddy Now

I know. You've heard it before. Had a dog. Loved it. Our companion during tough times. The dog got old, passed away. Heartbroken. Never again. It happens to someone every day. Friends suggest a new puppy, or a rescue dog but, "No, we never want to go through this again! Too painful!" Yep, that was us. My husband, Rob, and I.

We own a small acreage in Washington County, Texas, and for years used the small house there as a weekend retreat, a getaway from the fast pace of Houston. Our beautiful little Yorkie, ChanChan (née Chandler Bing, named by a then-teenage daughter and *Friends* enthusiast), went back and forth with us and became "ChanChan the Country Dog," as he loved to frolic in the rippling tall grass in the fields among the cows. He was a cute, affectionate little lap dog, and the recipient of lots of love and attention after our children were grown and left home. But Chan got old. Eventually he forgot his house-training. He was very stiff in the joints, and we weren't sure how much he could see or hear. He died in his sleep, and although we knew that his quality of life had decreased horribly and he was in a better place, we were heartbroken. Too painful. Never again.

But this is a story about Buddy. And Buddy was a real weirdo when we first met.

Rob and I had retired, sold our house in Houston, and built our forever home on our country property. We looked forward to living out our lives in our little paradise. And with no animals! No cleaning up after puppies, running them outside the second they started sniffing about, and no sopping up pee from an old dog who just couldn't hold it. Nope! Life was all new and shiny (as were our wood floors and unscratched doors), and totally under control. We didn't even plant a flower garden – something we had done for our entire adult lives. No weeds. No responsibilities.

EXCEPT, the first day in our new house, as we gazed out the window onto the patio and beyond, enjoying the idyllic view, there sat a little yellow dog. It seemed we had a squatter. He appeared to be an old dog, kind of ugly. He looked like a dingo. He was droopy from the heat. Oh no! A stray! We hoped he lived nearby and would just go on home.

I was very leery of him despite his diminutive size, having been attacked by a strange dog as a child. And this one looked wild… and filthy. He even had marks that looked to me like he had been shot with BBs, possibly the result of trying to make off with a neighbor's chicken or foraging in their trash. And who knew what diseases he might have!

We ignored him, hoping he'd just go home. That didn't work, so we fed him, leaving food and water out and going into the house so he would approach it (he was terrified of us). Our thinking was maybe he'd eat, feel better and have the energy to go home. No such luck. We advertised a found dog with his pathetic picture on Facebook and on placards we posted around the area. No takers. Rob checked with all of the neighbors. After a few days, I looked out and saw that the little dog was so weak from the heat and minimal eating, and he looked so sad.

"Rob," I said, "we have to trap this dog and take him to the shelter. This is no way for him to live!"

Now, remember, he was really people-shy. So catching him took some stealth. He'd eat and drink if we were nowhere around, but if anyone approached he headed for the hills. Of course, he always skulked back, taking up his post in the corner of the patio.

We had inadvertently named him Buddy. As in, "Go on home now, Buddy'" and then, "Come on Buddy, into the kennel," as we tried to lure him in with treats. Finally, he walked in when we were close enough to close the door.

Got him!, I thought with the tiniest tug at my heart.

It was a Monday morning in September. We put the kennel in the backseat of our truck and headed into town. Have I mentioned that Buddy had no voice? Not a peep, not a growl, not a bark, not a whine. He just sat there in the kennel and stared at me, and I felt like a heartless jerk. From the grim set of his jaw as he drove, I could tell Rob felt the same way.

We pulled up to the shelter. There was a sign on the door. The shelter had moved. I pulled out my phone and looked up the new address. It was closed on Mondays.

We sat there in the truck in the abandoned parking lot, contemplating what we should do. We looked at Buddy and then at each other. Okay, we agreed, if the vet's office was open, we'd at least have him checked for a chip and see if he was healthy. If everything checked out, we would think about keeping the little guy.

Of course, they were open! Of course, they could see us right away!

We carried the kennel with Buddy locked inside it into the office. Mind you, Buddy was still very spooky, and we had never even been able to touch him. We expressed our doubts about the dog to Dr. Boynton, and he said, "Well, let's see what we've got here."

He opened the kennel, and this wild dingo dog, who was terrified of people, became the perfect little gentleman. He walked out, sat, allowed the vet to poke, prod, and whatever else needed to be done in complete passivity. I'm sure Dr. Boynton thought we were crazy. Buddy was not chipped and he was perfectly healthy. To our surprise, we were told that he was only about six months old. When pressed, Dr. Boynton guessed that Buddy was part Chihuahua, part terrier, based on his size, pointy ears and nose and curly tail. So, after spending hundreds of dollars on shots, tests, flea medicine, a bed, and of course, treats, we took Buddy home.

As we drove home with Buddy sitting in his kennel in the backseat, seemingly listening to every word, we contemplated what this homely little guy may have been through in his short life. Had he been dropped off in the country by a disenchanted owner (this happens a lot), or had he wandered away from home? He obviously had received no love from humans, given his fear of people, brooms, and water hoses.

And so, the process began. I would go out to the patio every morning and sit in my chair while Buddy sat in the corner and watched me, both of us trying to overcome our trepidation. Eventually, he approached when offered a treat, and one day, he put his paws on my leg. I'll admit it, I nearly cried. I rubbed his paws and we began our friendship. Soon, he would come right to me and lay his head down on my leg to show me he trusted me. Oh, my heart!

Now, this dog was no ChanChan, with his soft, beautiful fur and darling teddy bear face. No, Buddy was all hard angles (except for his corkscrew tail), and stiff spiky fur that always seemed to have something sticky in it. Lord only knows what he found to roll in out there in the pasture. And he shed like a nervous cat. But he was full of personality and we came to adore him. He soon warmed up to Rob, came inside, and basically house-trained himself. He befriended our children and their spouses, and kept a respectful distance from our grandbabies.

He's part of the family. Our Bud Man. Our ride-or-die compadre, always ready for a run beside us in the golf cart, or a ride in the car to Houston to visit his girlfriend, Stella (my daughter's dog).

These days, while taking a break from tending to our amazing, prolifically blooming flower garden, Rob and I love to watch Buddy play. He lives to chase grasshoppers, hopping along after them. When he's happy, he prances like a Lipizzaner stallion. Although he refuses to fetch for us, he will toss his toys in the air, run after them, give them a shake, and toss them again. He will tear through the rippling tall grass of the hay meadow at full speed as though he is playing chase with someone. Maybe ChanChan the Country Dog has come back to play.

Buddy brought the love of a loyal companion back to us, and helped us heal when we didn't even know we needed healing. We'd like to think we've helped him heal a little too.

Debbie Schmitz

Debbie Schmitz is a writer, entrepreneur and former purveyor of antiques based in Central Texas. She has recently retired from her career as an antique store owner and now is devoted fulltime to her writing journey. Her works in process include a light-hearted mystery and a nonfiction guide in collaboration with her friend. Debbie lives with her husband Rob and their furry friends Buddy and Bill the Barn Cat. She also has three daughters and two grand-children.

Chapter Twenty-One

The War Dog

Wendy Rose Williams

Indie camping with her Mom Aki Nguyen (Dusty Lake, Washington)

"*Y*ou can call me Bella!" she announced enthusiastically.

I was astonished by how well I could hear the dog I planned to adopt, yet I hesitated, concerned that my senior cat Midnight might not accept the four-year old Shepherd mix the way he had agreed to the timid, young male pocket boxer mix we'd originally requested. But the moment I saw Bella's stark shelter photo, I heard, *Foster her. It's important you help save her life.*

The Saturday before Thanksgiving, I headed to pick up my dog from the Dog Gone Seattle Rescue. My contact, Jenny, had mentioned that almost thirty dogs were arriving due to severe overcrowding at the California shelter. Dogs needed to be rescued immediately or they would be euthanized. An estimated 5,500 dogs are killed daily in the U.S. shelters per An Act of Dog's Museum of Compassion. (See an ActofDog.org for more information.)

Those of us in rescue see too many impulse purchases; people underestimate the amount of daily work, training and exercise required for responsible dog ownership and not enough dogs are being spayed and neutered. There's also a backyard breeder profit incentive and the issue of neglect. These factors all lead to dogs being dumped at the shelters through no fault of their own.

I parked and easily spotted Jenny, who, with clipboard and dog collars in hand was matching each dog coming off the van to its host family. It was remarkable how quickly this Dog-Whisperer bonded with each pup as she crouched down and spoke with him or her. She expertly ran her hands over each dog, assessing health and temperament, while checking for ticks.

I also *recognized* Jenny immediately, though we had never met. She was beautiful, despite wearing no makeup, a messy pony-tail and cargo pants covered in dog hair and muddy paw prints.

Jenny's image changed to another time and place. I remembered us helping animals together in other lifetimes, including as brothers in England. We saved as many foxes as we could from the cruel "sport" of hunting with hounds on horseback.

I sensed several lives with Jenny. My Guides had been specific during multiple meditations, that I was to volunteer in dog rescue, specifically with Jenny and her husband Jon. I sensed a soul contract made with each of them before we incarnated.

I had a sinking feeling something had gone terribly wrong in one of my lives with Jenny. My Guides had commented, *What happened was unforgivable. You need to make it right the best you can. Love and care for her to the best of your ability – help her help the dogs!*

I snapped back to the present when my name was called. Bella stepped confidently off the van, a beautiful light-colored Shepherd with an intelligent look in her eyes.

The moment I began walking Bella, I discovered to my surprise I had no game. She was clearly walking me, and my left knee began to buckle and feel strange, though I didn't have knee problems.

When I asked Jenny for dog-walking pointers, she demonstrated loose-leash walking and how to redirect by turning quickly in the other direction if the dog was not following my lead. Bella walked remarkably better with Jenny who was not only an expert, but taller and stronger as well as twenty years younger than me.

Jenny reminded me to have Bella drag a leash at home for the first few days and decompress in her crate. She was also not to meet my other animals for several days.

When we arrived home, I took Bella for a long walk, hoping to tire her out before crating her. My left leg felt increasingly odd.

I put Bella back in the car, praying she wouldn't eat my upholstery. Then, after securing Midnight, I fed Bella, gave her water and put her in the crate in my master bathroom. I began to slowly back out of the room, telling the dog firmly to STAY, ignoring her barking and whining.

An explosion of black hissing fur catapulted past my legs and charged the crate. Midnight had managed to pull down the latch on the closed bedroom door and push it open, and had now bolted past me when I opened the bathroom door.

Bella took one look at this Tasmanian Devil and burst out of her crate, breaking the zip-ties I'd added for reinforcement. The crate flew in different directions and the warring cat and dog were in full physical contact.

There was no time to get something to separate them, and instinct told me to keep my face and hands above the melee. I took a deep breath, pulled my sweatshirt over my hands and shoved my way in between the howling pair. I hip-checked the dog hard to my left into the vanity. Bella lifted her head in surprise which allowed me to grab her collar and haul her quickly from the bathroom. I threw a towel over the cat to slow him down in case he gave chase and slammed the door firmly behind us.

Bella and I lurched into the Great Room, adrenalin pumping. My left calf was throbbing but before I could examine it Spike, our rabbit, raced across the back porch.

Bella taught me an immediate lesson in prey drive. I had to tackle her to stop her from going through the French doors to get to Spike. I was petrified she was going to get out of her collar, yank the leash out of my hands or break through the glass doors. This wasn't what I'd pictured when I got a dog to get more exercise. This was insane. This was war!

I hauled Bella out the front door, heart pounding, and after a few moments of rest took her on another walk. My left leg was still bleeding from the bite on the back of my calf, but fortunately, my thick socks and new jeans had provided some protection.

When we got home I put a resistant Bella back in my car again, then placed Spike in his hutch on the back porch and Midnight in an upstairs bedroom. I retrieved Bella from my car, and kept her with me as I cooked dinner. It was easy to do as she glued herself to my left side, which felt so familiar.

I tried to watch TV with Bella, but every time she began to relax, the cat would rattle the bedroom door in its frame. With each howl and hiss, the dog would bark and scramble to her feet in response, and it was all I could do to hold onto her. My home felt like a battleground.

Now in tears, I called Jenny for the third time to learn that every foster home was full. The boarding facility the rescue used occasionally had closed for the weekend. I might be able to take Bella to Jenny's the next day if space became available. But first we had to get through the night.

The best plan I could come up with was for Bella and I to sleep in my car. I placed her new dog beds and blanket in the cargo area, then made myself as comfortable as possible on the bench back seat. Thankfully, we both fell asleep quickly.

That night, I dreamed about sleeping with Bella on my left side, my weapon was on my right. We'd done it for so many months decades earlier it was a muscle memory in my current body. My left knee throbbed – I knew my left lower leg and foot were gone, but the phantom pain was excruciating. What was happening? I kept hearing *past life release*.

I woke up a few hours later sobbing. I felt gutted by the depth of emotion from innumerable soldiers surrounding us. The soldiers were Earth-bound souls – ghosts – who hadn't passed to the Light after their deaths. But why were they *here*? I was a Ghost-Whisperer, but I couldn't walk this many Home – the numbers were overwhelming.

I called on the soul of a beloved actor friend who had crossed over a few years earlier and was a genius at helping stuck souls get to the Light. But countless more soldiers poured in, gutting me with their pain and heartbreak. I sensed a portal had opened on my property. Most of the soldiers looked like they were from World War II, but some were from earlier wars and some from conflicts as recent as Afghanistan.

I knew my spiritual teacher Birdie had built a portal for these soldiers to get Home. I told my Guides firmly I was NOT willing to host this portal on my property as there was too much grief to transmute. I sensed my actor/ comedian friend begin to lead the soldiers and suicides west toward the Olympic Peninsula, while cheerfully bellowing, "Good Morning, Vietnam!"

I fell back into an uneasy sleep. No amount of shifting restored the feeling in my left leg and foot. My left leg felt blown away. I was still limping badly the next morning when I fed the three animals, then texted an SOS to Birdie. She called a few moments later and quickly helped me put the pieces together.

"Did Bella have a different name when you got her? It feels like you have a past life together. That's part of this intense energy you're both releasing. Your property looks like a war zone when I tune into it clairvoyantly. It's energetically blown up all around you."

"I know! I can't transmute this much energy – more and more soldiers keep pouring in, and they need help. Bella's name is technically Berlin."

"What kind of dog is she? Her soul is incredibly brave – she feels like your war dog."

"She's a German Shepherd mix. What does that have to do with – Oh my God! You're right. I see our life together now. I was a young American soldier sent to Berlin during World War II. Berlin's in Germany – this dog's name is BERLIN, and she's a GERMAN

Shepherd! Talk about past life clues – it's so obvious now – it feels like something bad happened to my leg."

"Yes. You and Berlin were inseparable during the war. She's practically glued to your left leg trying to protect you. She saved your life – I see her dragging you by your shirt and arm out of a building that's on fire – you're unconscious. You stepped on something with your left foot – there was an explosion. It looks like your leg had to be amputated above the knee. How's your leg now?"

I was openly sobbing. "I can't feel my left leg or foot. It's like it's not there and my knee keeps buckling. This past life energy is so intense in combination with all these ghosts. Did I open a portal last night by mistake while I was sleeping?"

"Yes, you did. You and Berlin went back to that lifetime together in a big way to release the war energy, not only for yourselves but for mankind. We'll finish relocating the portal in a minute and restore peace."

"Now I feel even worse that I can't keep this amazing dog after she saved my life. Do you see any way I can adopt her?"

"No, Midnight won't agree to it, but you don't need to keep her. You transmuted your karma with Berlin when you agreed to take her. She saved your life during World War II and now you've saved hers. I feel she's going to attract her forever home quickly. Let's finish moving that portal off your property – our actor friend can help with that." She paused. "Do you know why he's bellowing 'Good Morning, Vietnam?'"

I laughed. "I've heard him do that since the day he went Home. It helps lighten the mood as he calls in the soldiers. It's a clarion call, so they know where to go to find the Light."

"He's amazingly loud – it's why so many ghosts are coming in. Okay, it's working – the portal on your property is closed. He's leading them to the portal over the Strait of Juan de Fuca by Port Angeles. Angels are coming in to help because there are so many ghosts around you and your war dog. You need to ground and clear your energy and be sovereign – don't let the soldiers in your energy field anymore. You can't process this much emotion on their behalf. No one can. They'll heal at Home."

"Birdie, I so appreciate your help!"

"You're welcome. Berlin has been both a stellar war dog as well as a war horse for many people in her different incarnations. She deserves a wonderful life. I feel she's going to get it now. Great job finding one another and healing this old energy!"

After a bittersweet morning with my dog, I packed up her things and drove her to Jenny's. It was hard not to burst into tears as Jenny graciously welcomed Berlin and got her settled in a crate in the living room, but I knew she'd be matched with the best possible home. It was time to let her go.

That day, I asked Jenny if I could help the rescue other than by fostering or adopting, and was soon volunteering at adoption events, with transport, at Intake (arrivals) and with fundraising events. Berlin, I was thrilled to hear, was quickly adopted by her new foster family after spending a few days with Jenny. She was renamed Indie, loves to hike and camp, and is now living her best life! I couldn't ask for more for my brave War Dog.

Three years after meeting Berlin, my left leg finally healed from my traumatic past life injury. I had waded up to my knees in the frigid red spring water at the Glastonbury Chalice Well & Gardens in England. My intermittent limp is gone, and my left leg no longer buckles under me.

Dog Gone Seattle is a 501c3 organization. It is the largest foster-based rescue in Washington State, having saved over 800 dogs from euthanasia in 2019. This 100% volunteer organization works tirelessly to change the reality for the thousands of dogs a day who are not as fortunate as Berlin. Visit DogGoneSeattle.org to learn how you can help.

Wendy Rose Williams

Wendy Rose Williams is a Past Life Adventure Guide who helps people from around the world release negative experiences they're unconsciously carrying forward. When they become consciously aware of this energy it releases pain, anxiety and depression so that they can lead happy, healthy active lives filled with purpose. She helps people release energy that no longer serves them, regardless if that energy is from last week, last year, childhood or from a past life.

Wendy trained with Dr. Brian Weiss ('*Many Lives, Many Masters*') for past-life regression. She is a Reiki Master Energy Healer, Certified Spiritual Teacher, channel for Mary Magdalen, author and speaker, as well as a Hypnotherapist. Wendy lives on Seattle's Eastside and works with clients from around the world via teleconference call.

She is an active volunteer with the Dog Gone Seattle Rescue. Her most devoted writing partner remains her cat Midnight. Her books are available on Amazon and in audio book format on Audible.

Request your complimentary phone appointment with Wendy via her website:

https://www.wendyrosewilliams.com/
Email: Wendy@WendyRoseWilliams.com
https://www.facebook.com/gwendolyn.rose.79
Instagram: WilliamsWendyRose

Chapter Twenty-Two

Wally

Gail "GG" Rush Gould

Wally

*W*ally was rescued on the side of Route 1, along with his brothers and sisters and their mom, who was tied to the guard rail. A sad start to life. I was separated, broke, and my daughters and I were still grieving the loss of Rosie, our purebred Sheltie. Luckily, for both us and Wally, things were about to take a turn for the better.

I have always had a dog in my life, the first of which was a terrier named Dino. Others followed throughout my childhood, and when I became an adult there was Honey, a Shepard Golden Retriever mix that I picked up at the pound. Honey was with me through my wedding and the birth of both my girls, and she was my best friend until she had a stroke and couldn't walk. Putting her to sleep broke my heart but it was the right thing to end her suffering.

Rosie came next, a gift from my parents to the girls. She was bred to be a show dog but was too large for the breed; she was also neurotic and afraid of everything. But she loved those girls, and we loved her. She died in my arms in the middle of the night after suffering a heart attack. It was one of the worst moments of my life.

After that I told the girls we would wait a while before getting another dog; I just couldn't bear the thought of going through that pain again. That resolve lasted about three months. I realized I needed a dog and so did my girls. We missed coming home to unconditional love and affection. That's how we ended up at the adoption event hosted by the organization that had saved Wally and his family. That day the adoption fee was seventy-five dollars and included shots and spay or neuter. I had, by some twist of fate, exactly that amount in my pocket, saved from several paychecks, probably to be sure I could pay the electric bill.

There were three puppies in a playpen, all golden in color, all rather funny-looking. The best guess the adoption people had was that they were a basset and lab mix. The female was spoken for, and a boy and his parents were deciding which of the two males – one of which was kind of plump – they would choose. As we watched them debate, one of my daughters said she wanted "the fat one" and the other daughter favored the other. Finally, the boy scooped up the fat one and promptly named him Bart. So we grabbed the last one. Wally. He fell asleep in my daughter's arms on the way home. The inseparable bond had been instantly formed.

For the first several months Wally was nothing short of a terror. He was growing fast and he was strong. He ate furniture. I began to think I'd made a mistake. But the girls were attached to him, and so was I. In time he settled down. And he was adorable, with his short little turned-out basset legs and his long Retriever body and golden fur. He had floppy basset ears that were softer than velvet. His nature was gentle and laid back. He was loved by all the neighbors, adults and kids alike. Whenever we walked around the block people would stop what they were doing to greet him.

Wally ruled the roost. When my younger daughter brought home a kitten one night from Girl Scouts, I said, "If Wally doesn't like her she goes back." But Wally tolerated her and even grew to love her. Wally and the kitten, who we name Bella, became best buddies. They played together and napped together.

For fourteen years, Wally watched his little girls grow into young women. He went through braces and proms and college. I cried silently into his neck when I was getting divorced. He didn't judge me. He just loved me.

Two months ago, on a hundred-degree day, our boy collapsed in the backyard. I had just come home from work and I let him out as always. He walked a few feet and just fell over. He couldn't get up. My daughter came home and we couldn't lift him. I covered him with a wet towel to keep him cool and my daughter cradled his head in her lap.

I frantically tried to reach a mobile vet, but it was the week of July 4th and no one was responding. I called a friend and he and my daughter were able to roll Wally onto a blanket and get him in my car. My daughter and I drove him to the emergency vet, where they determined that his spleen had ruptured. He was in pain and confused. He would not recover. My daughter and I knew we couldn't let him suffer any longer. Together we stroked his soft ears and told him how much we loved him as he peacefully went to sleep.

The next day I went out to the backyard to put some garbage in the can. I was thinking about Wally and how much we already missed him. Suddenly, I was surrounded by dragonflies. Lots of dragonflies. I felt Wally's spirit was letting me know he was at peace. It was a beautiful moment. A month later I put in a pollinator garden near where Wally had collapsed. I placed a statue of a dog with wings, that looks remarkably like Wally, in that garden. And now, literally every day, there is a dragonfly circling that statue, reminding us that our friend is still there, comforting and loving us.

Thank you, Wally, for all you have given our family. We will love you forever.

Gail "GG" Rush Gould

Gail "GG" Rush Gould is a perpetual student and seeker of knowledge, experience and enlightenment. She is a "Wayfinder Life Coach In-Training" and attended Martha Beck's African Star Program at Londolozi Game Reserve in South Africa. She is certified in Reiki II as well as studying Aromatherapy and learning the ancient art of Pulse Reading. GG has traveled the world solo and is currently working on a book about her journeys and self-discovery. She resides in Cary, North Carolina with her cat Bella.

Animal Charities Dear to Our Hearts

Patriot Dog Assistance Program

http://www.patriotassistancedogs.org

Orphans of the Storm Rescue Center

https://orphansofthestorm.org

Friend for Life Animal Rescue

https://azfriends.org

Farm Sanctuary

https://www.farmsanctuary.org

Guiding Eyes for the Blind

https://www.guidingeyes.org

Horse Whiskey Rescue

http://www.horsewhiskeyrescue.org

True Blue Animal Rescue

http://www.t-bar.org

Live Like Roo

https://livelikeroo.org

Daphney Land Basset Hound Rescue
http://www.daphneyland.com

New England Society for Abandoned Animals
https://www.nesaa.org

Birdhouse Doghouse Rescue Foundation
https://m.facebook.com/operationlovemarylea

Dog Gone Seattle Rescue
https://www.doggoneseattle.org

ASPCA
https://www.aspca.org

Dog Ranch Rescue
https://www.dogranchrescue.com

Dachshund Rescue of North America
https://www.drna.org

Your Book. Your Vision. Your Way.

Transcendent Publishing
P.O. Box 66202
St. Pete Beach, FL 33736
800.232.5087

www.transcendentpublishing.com

CPSIA information can be obtained
at www.ICGtesting.com
Printed in the USA
FFHW010828230120
57937420-63131FF